ALASKA Roadhouse Recipes

Memorable recipes from roadhouses, lodges,
bed and breakfasts, cafés, restaurants and campgrounds
along the highways and byways of Alaska and Canada

From the Editors of The MILEPOST®

Vernon Publications Inc.

Photography: All photos courtesy of the recipe contributors, with the exception of those listed below.
Jerrianne Lowther, pages 55, 107, 113, 118, 129, 171, 181, 207, 214; Earl L. Brown, pages 20, 27, 51, 82, 103, 116, 194; Sharon Nault, pages 4, 7, 59, 65, 91; Judy Parkin, page 198. Mary Carey photo on page 60 courtesy of "The Frontiersman/Valley Sun."

Cover Photo: Chef Greybeard of Alaska Wildland Adventures shows off his Skilak Omelet. (Photo courtesy of Alaska Wildland Adventures)

Recipes were solicited from the contributors. Recipes were reviewed by editors and in some cases tested, but the publisher offers no guarantee of individual results.

Design: David L. Ranta
Editor: Kris Graef
Editorial Assistant: Michelle Arab
Food Consultant: Judy Vernon
Production Manager: Barton R. Vernon
Fulfillment Manager: Tina L. Boyle
Associate Publisher: Michele Andrus Dill
Publisher: Geoffrey P. Vernon

Publisher of: The MILEPOST®, ALASKA A to Z, NORTHWEST MILEPOSTS®, The ALASKA WILDERNESS GUIDE, The MILEPOST® Souvenir Logbook

ISBN 1-878425-59-5
Key title: Alaska Roadhouse Recipes
Printed in U.S.A. on recyclable stock.

Vernon Publications Inc. 🗡
3000 Northup Way, Suite 200
Bellevue, WA 98004-1446
(206) 827-9900
1-800-726-4707
Fax (206) 822-9372
E-mail: books@alaskainfo.com
Internet address: www.alaskainfo.com

CONTENTS

Breakfasts   7

Appetizers   51

Beverages   59

Breads   65

Soups, Salads & Side Dishes   107

Main Dishes   129

Desserts   171

Sauces, Syrups & Preserves   207

Contributors   216

Index   221

P hoto of the old Sourdough Roadhouse, located at Mile 147.5 Richardson Highway, was taken in the early 1980s. The historic structure offered gas, food and lodging to highway travelers until it burned down in December 1992.

INTRODUCTION

Roadhouse. In the North, this term refers to those early-day hostelries along the trails used by dog-team, horse-drawn sled and wagon stage. Spaced about a day's journey apart (by horse or by dog), the roadhouse offered food and shelter to everyone from miners to missionaries.

Today, roadhouse means the same as lodge, hotel, bed and breakfast, or campground. It is an outpost of hospitality in a very large land. The modern-day equivalents of those early-day roadhouses offer that same Northern hospitality: a place to stay and a good meal for their guests. Many of these modern-day hosts have generously shared their recipes with us, from the hotel chef's haute cuisine to the roadhouse cook's more basic grub.

Of the hundreds of roadhouses in the early days of the North, relatively few remain. Many have simply vanished, while the ruins of others may be seen along the road. These include the old Black Rapids Lodge, described as the "farthest north of the old-time Richardson trail hostelries," which is still visible along the Richardson Highway. The Central Roadhouse site, on the National Register of Historic Places, may be seen from the Steese Highway near Central, Alaska.

A few roadhouses became private homes. Others housed different businesses over the years, more often than not a bar. Fire has claimed many old structures, such as the Sourdough Roadhouse and the Richardson Roadhouse. The Blix Roadhouse in Copper Center, Alaska, which operated during the gold rush days of 1897-1898, was destroyed by fire, but was replaced by the Copper Center Lodge in 1932.

Other roadhouses and lodges—Paxson, Manley, Talkeetna, Gakona, Eureka, Sheep Mountain, Tiekel River and Tsaina, to name a few—have survived, and continue to offer travelers a warm bed and a hot meal on a cold night. These survivors have been renovated, and sometimes completely rebuilt, but they retain the spirit of the original roadhouse.

Diana Graf of Rika's Roadhouse, which is now part of a state historical park, writes: "Roadhouses smelled of fireplace wood and moose hide. Pioneers and visitors swapped stories in warm parlors, where there were big, creaking rocking chairs and tables littered with long-out-of-date magazines. Meals were served at long tables covered with oil cloth and there were beaten paths outside leading to the outhouses."

Indoor plumbing has pretty much replaced the outhouses, but the shared warmth of the fire, the shared meal and the shared stories among travelers can still be found among the hostelries of the North.

This collection of recipes salutes the hosts of the North and their businesses, whether they date back a century or a decade; whether they are roadhouses, bed and breakfasts or campgrounds; whether they are found along the historic Richardson Highway in Alaska, the Klondike Highway in Yukon, or the Yellowhead Highway in British Columbia. Eat and enjoy!

Breakfasts

stablished in 1903, the Sourdough Roadhouse was approved as a historical site by the state of Alaska in the spring of 1974 and became a national historic landmark in 1979. It was the oldest roadhouse in Alaska still operating in the original building until it burned down in December 1992. The roadhouse was located at Mile 147.5 Richardson Highway. When it was still in business, the Sourdough Roadhouse advertised "family atmosphere, good home-cooked food" and a "sourdough breakfast anytime." Some outbuildings remain, and nearby a portion of the old Valdez trail is still visible. Used by gold stampeders to the Klondike in 1898, the Valdez trail led from the port of Valdez to Eagle. It was later converted to a wagon road and eventually became today's Richardson Highway.

ALMOST FAMOUS GRANOLA

Wenda Lythgoe & Brent Liddle, The Cabin Bed & Breakfast
Km 219 Haines Highway

"You can leave out or add in any other suitable granola ingredients to your liking. You can also increase or decrease any of the ingredients. Make it your own!"

5 cups old-fashioned oats
5 cups regular oats
1 cup raw bran
¹/₂ to 1 cup oat bran and/or wheat germ
¹/₂ to ³/₄ cup brown sugar
1 cup sunflower seeds
1 cup sesame seeds
1 cup pumpkin seeds
2 Tb. flax seeds
¹/₂ cup skim-milk powder
2 cups chopped nuts (I use sliced almonds and pecans)
1 cup unsweetened ribbon coconut
¹/₂ cup frozen orange juice or apple juice concentrate
¹/₂ cup water
¹/₂ cup vegetable oil
¹/₂ to 1 cup honey
1 Tb. vanilla
1 to 2 tsp. (or to taste) cinnamon, nutmeg OR ginger, optional
1 cup dried fruit

Start with the oats in a large mixing bowl. Add next 10 ingredients. In a saucepan, combine juice, water, oil, honey, vanilla and optional spices. Heat gently to melt honey and mix ingredients. Pour slowly over granola and mix well to coat evenly. Put in 9" x 13" baking pans or larger size, approximately 1 inch deep. Bake, uncovered, at 325°F for 30 minutes or until lightly browned. Stir every 5 to 10 minutes, and more frequently towards the end of baking, to prevent the granola on the edges of pan from burning. Remove from oven.

Add 1 cup chopped, dried fruit (raisins, apples, apricots, peaches, etc.) and let cool, stirring occasionally. Store in an airtight container in a cool place, or it keeps in the freezer for months. Makes approximately 20 cups.

GOOD MORNING GRANOLA

Jon and Nelda Osgood
Tutka Bay Wilderness Lodge, Homer

6 cups **rolled oats**
1 cup **wheat germ, untoasted**
1 cup **sesame seeds**
1 cup **sunflower seeds**
1 cup **shredded coconut**
1 cup **sliced almonds**
1 cup **dried fruit (raisins, cranberries, dates, apricots, etc.)**
1 cup **nonfat dry milk**
1 cup **oil**
1 cup **honey**

Preheat the oven to 300°F. In a large bowl, combine all of the dry ingredients. Drizzle the oil and honey over the dry ingredients and mix very well. Spread the mixture on a large baking sheet, and toast in the oven for 30 to 40 minutes, stirring every 10 minutes. Remove mixture from the oven when it is lightly browned. If it gets too brown, it will taste burned. Cool completely and store refrigerated in an airtight container. Granola will keep for several weeks. Makes 15 cups, or enough for 30 1/2-cup servings.

HELGA'S HOT CEREAL

Helga Garrison, Helga's B&B, Sitka

"The dish needs to be prepared the night before, or it won't taste right."

1¹/₂ cups of milk (or more if needed)
2 cups cooked, firm rice (do not use instant rice)
1 cup diced, dry apricots
2 unpeeled apples, diced
1 cup raisins
1 tsp. cinnamon
¹/₂ tsp. cloves
2 eggs

The night before, mix all of the ingredients together in a large bowl. It will be very thin. Put in a 9" x 13" baking pan (that is sprayed with nonstick spray). In the morning, dot with butter, if you wish. Bake at 375°F for 45 minutes. Serve plain or with toast. Can also be eaten cold as a snack later in the day. Serves 8.

BAKED APPLE PANCAKE

Sharon Waisanen, Spruce Avenue Bed & Breakfast
Soldotna

"The Finnish name for this pancake is 'Omenapannukakku.' Our son, Kyle, has requested this pancake for years as his favorite. Our guests love it, too."

4 eggs	3 large apples, peeled,
1¹/₂ cups milk	cored and sliced
¹/₂ tsp. salt	cinnamon sugar (¹/₂ cup sugar and
2 Tb. sugar mixed with	3 tsp. cinnamon)
2 cups sifted white flour	whipped cream (or whipped topping)

Beat eggs well; add milk, salt and sugar. Sift in flour, mixing it well. Let the batter stand for 30 minutes. Butter well two 8- or 9-inch round cake pans (or a 9" x 13" rectangular pan), and sprinkle with part of the cinnamon sugar. Arrange the sliced apples in the pans. Sprinkle the apples with cinnamon sugar (save some of the sugar to sprinkle over the batter). Pour the pancake batter over the apples, dividing it evenly between the pans. Sprinkle with remaining cinnamon sugar.

Bake in a moderately hot oven (375°F) for about 30 minutes or until the top of pancake is golden and set. This is best served immediately, but can be reheated before serving. Serve plain or with cream (or whipped topping). We also serve it with rhubarb, lingonberry or raspberry jam. Serves 2 to 4.

BANANA NUT PANCAKES

Kim Kirby, Millar Street House Bed & Breakfast
Ketchikan

"Guests at our B&B always enjoy these pancakes, which we serve when the skies are grey and Ketchikan is receiving just some of its 13 feet of rain. They seem to give the energy required to take on the day."

1¹/₂ **cups sifted all-purpose flour**
1 **tsp. salt**
3 **Tb. sugar**
1³/₄ **tsp. baking powder**
1 **slightly beaten egg**
3 **Tb. melted butter**
1 **to** 1¹/₄ **cups milk**
1 **mashed banana**
¹/₂ **cup chopped pecans**

Sift together flour, salt, sugar and baking powder. In a separate bowl, combine egg, butter, milk, banana and pecans. Mix the liquid ingredients with the dry ingredients swiftly and let rest for 10 minutes. Cook by spooning mixture onto a hot griddle for about 2 to 3 minutes on each side. Serve with hot maple syrup and butter. Serves 6.

"DREAM" OVEN PANCAKE

Sharon Waisanen, Spruce Avenue Bed & Breakfast
Soldotna

"The Finnish name for this pancake is 'Unelemapannukakku.' We like topping this pancake with homemade blueberry jam, whipped cream and slices of kiwi fruit."

1 cup whipping cream
2 eggs
2 Tb. sugar
¹/₂ cup sifted white flour
1¹/₂ Tb. melted butter

Whip the cream until stiff, and set aside. Beat together the eggs and sugar until very light. Fold in half of the whipped cream. Sift the flour over the cream/egg mixture, fold it in well, then fold in the melted butter. Pour into a well-buttered 8- or 9-inch flan pan (or round cake pan) and bake at 375°F for 15 minutes. Top with jam, the remaining whipped cream and fresh fruit slices before serving. Serves 2.

FINNISH OVEN PANCAKE

Sharon Waisanen, Spruce Avenue Bed & Breakfast
Soldotna

4 eggs
2 Tb. sugar
2³/₄ cups milk
1 tsp. salt
1³/₄ cups flour

Preheat oven to 425°F.
Beat eggs and sugar well. Add milk and salt. Gradually add flour, beating until thoroughly mixed. Butter a 9" x 13" pan. Pour in batter. Bake for 20 to 25 minutes. Serve with jam, syrup or fresh fruit, and/or whipped topping.

GINGERBREAD PANCAKES WITH LEMON CURD

Judy Urquhart, Blueberry Lodge Bed and Breakfast
Juneau

"This is the most requested recipe at Blueberry Lodge B&B."

2¹/₂ cups **flour**
5 tsp. **baking powder**
1 tsp. **baking soda**
1¹/₂ tsp. **salt**
1 tsp. **cinnamon**
¹/₂ tsp. **ginger**
2 **eggs**
2 cups **milk**

¹/₄ cup **molasses**
1 cup **raisins**

Lemon Curd:
3 **eggs**
¹/₂ cup **sugar**
²/₃ cup **lemon juice**
6 Tb. **melted butter**
zest of lemon (optional)

In a large bowl, combine flour, baking powder, baking soda, salt, cinnamon and ginger. In a separate bowl, beat eggs slightly, then stir in milk and molasses. Pour egg mixture into dry ingredients. Stir only until moistened. Stir in raisins. Pour pancakes onto griddle. Flip when bubbles show through. Serve with syrup and lemon curd. Serves 5 to 6.

For lemon curd, combine eggs, sugar and lemon juice. Add melted butter and mix well. Microwave on low, stirring with whisk every 2 minutes, until thick. Stir in lemon zest. Serve warm on top of pancakes.

OVERNIGHT SOURDOUGH PANCAKES

Ked Schoming, Morning Glory B&B, Homer

2 cups **warm water**
1 tsp. **yeast, at room temperature**
2 cups **flour**
1 tsp. **salt**
2 Tb. **sugar**
1 Tb. **oil**
1 **egg**
1 tsp. **baking soda**

The night before, mix yeast in warm water until dissolved. Mix flour and yeast together. Cover and let sit in a warm place overnight. (Important: Do not use a metal pan or spoon.)

The next morning, mix salt, sugar, oil, egg and baking soda with yeast and flour mixture to desired consistancy (add water for thinner batter) and cook on a 350°F grill. Makes 18 medium-size pancakes.

SAUSAGE OVEN PANCAKE

Sharon Waisanen, Spruce Avenue Bed & Breakfast
Soldotna

"The main recipes we use at our B&B are all Finnish oven pancakes. This is a Finnish recipe known as 'Makkarapannukakku.'"

2 eggs
1¹/₂ cups milk
1¹/₂ cups white flour
1 tsp. baking powder
1 tsp. salt
¹/₂ lb. sausage (I use ham slices or reindeer sausage)
1 small onion, sliced
¹/₂ cup shredded cheddar cheese

eat the eggs well. Add milk, flour, baking powder and salt. Butter a 9" x 13" pan well. Arrange slices of sausage and onions in layers. Pour pancake batter over, then sprinkle the cheese evenly over the batter. Bake at 400°F for about 20 minutes or until golden brown. Serve with jam, syrup, fresh fruit or whipped topping. Serves 2 to 4.

SWEDISH OVEN PANCAKE

Camp Denali and North Face Lodge
Denali National Park

"Resembling a large popover, this breakfast dish is impressive when served at the table from a cast iron skillet. It must come directly from the oven, as it will gradually fall. We recommend a topping of lingonberry sauce and yogurt. Commercial whole cranberry sauce may be substituted for lingonberries."

3 strips bacon	**1 cup flour**
3 eggs	**2 Tb. sugar**
2 cups milk	**1/2 tsp. salt**

Cut bacon up and brown it until crisp in a 12- or 13-inch-diameter frying pan.* Do not pour off drippings. Beat eggs and milk together lightly, or combine in a blender. Add flour, sugar and salt, and blend together only until ingredients are combined. Do not overmix. Reheat pan with bacon drippings, and then pour in batter. It should sizzle when added to the pan. Bake in a preheated 375°F oven until lightly browned and puffed (30 minutes). Bring to the table immediately, cut and serve with fruit or berry preserves, syrup or fresh-squeezed lemon juice and a dusting of powdered sugar. Serves 4 to 5.

*A smaller frying pan can be used, and the bacon and drippings transferred to the equivalent of a 9" x 13" baking pan. Reheat pan and drippings before adding batter.

MOOSE CREEK SOURDOUGH PANCAKES

Don and Joanne Lefler, Moose Creek Lodge
Mile 229.1 Klondike Highway

2²/₃ cups **flour**

4 Tb. **sugar**

2 Tb. **baking powder**

2 tsp. **salt**

2 **eggs**

1¹/₄ cups **milk**

1¹/₄ cups **sourdough starter**
(see recipe following)

1¹/₄ cups **water**

6 Tb. **oil**

¹/₂ tsp. **vanilla**

Combine flour, sugar, baking powder and salt, and set aside. In separate bowl, combine eggs, milk, starter, water, oil and vanilla, and mix thoroughly. Add dry ingredients. Cook by spooning mixture onto a hot griddle for about 2 to 3 minutes on each side. Serves 6 to 8.

Sourdough Starter

1 cup flour
1 cup warm water
1 package active dry yeast
1 Tb. sugar

Mix the ingredients thoroughly in a gallon jar (to allow room to triple). Let mix stand, loosely covered, for a day or two, until it is frothy and full of bubbles. The bubbling will begin shortly after you mix the ingredients, but it will take a longer time for the bubbles to permeate the mixture and for the sour smell of sourdough to develop.

After mixture has fermented and soured, stir it down and refrigerate. It will be better after it has aged a few days in the refrigerator. Replenish after each use.

To replenish starter, replace equal amounts of flour and water according to amount of starter used (for example, if you use 1 cup of starter, replace with 1 cup of flour and 1 cup of water), stir and return to fridge.

TREEHOUSE SIGNATURE SOURDOUGH PANCAKES

Jessie Marrs, Alaska's Treehouse Bed & Breakfast, Seward

The sourdough starter used in this pancake recipe needs to sit for 5 days. Serve these pancakes with Lowbush Cranberry Butter (see recipe under Sauces, Syrups & Preserves).

2¹/₂ cups **flour**
2 cups **warm water**
1 cup **sourdough starter (see recipe following)**
¹/₄ cup **powdered skim milk**
1 **egg**
2 Tb. **sugar**
1 tsp. **salt**
1 tsp. **baking soda**

The night before mix flour with the warm water and add starter. Stir well and cover with a damp cloth. In the morning, take out 1 cup of starter and reserve for future use (store in refrigerator). Add powdered milk and egg to remaining batter, beating well. Combine sugar, salt and baking soda; sprinkle evenly over batter, then fold in gently. Let batter rest a few minutes. Cook on a hot, oiled griddle. Serves 4.

Sourdough Starter

1 Tb. dry yeast
2¹/₂ cups warm water
2 tsp. sugar OR honey
2¹/₂ cups flour

Mix together ingredients and let ferment 5 days at room temperature, stirring daily. Starter will keep indefinitely in the refrigerator, but should be used once a week.

BAKED PEACH FRENCH TOAST

James G. Beard, Arctic Fox Inn, Anchorage

1 large loaf **unsliced French bread**
8 **eggs, well beaten**
6 cups **whole or 2% milk**
1/2 cup **brown sugar**
1 Tb. **vanilla**
1 large can **sliced peaches**
2 cups **whipping cream**
1 **whole fresh nutmeg, grated just before serving**

lice French bread into thick slices and leave unwrapped overnight to harden. Beat eggs and milk with sugar and vanilla. Soak bread slices thoroughly and grill over medium heat until lightly crusty. Place overlapping in baking dishes and surround with peach slices. Bake at 350°F for 30 minutes. Whip cream while French toast is baking. Decorate edge of pan with whipped cream and grate fresh nutmeg over all. Serve immediately. Serves 12.

FOTZELSCHNITTEN (SWISS FRENCH TOAST)

Brigitte Suter
Brigitte's Bavarian Bed & Breakfast, Homer

1/4 **cup milk**
4 eggs
salt
nutmeg
8 stale slices **brown bread**
3 Tb. **butter**
plum jam, applesauce OR maple syrup

eat the milk in a small saucepan, until warm. Beat the eggs, adding salt and nutmeg to taste in a separate bowl. Stick the bread slices on a fork, and dip first in the milk and then in the eggs. Melt a part of the butter in a fry pan. Add 2 to 3 slices of bread and fry until golden brown on both sides. Put in warm place and proceed in the same way with the rest of the bread. Serve with plum jam, applesauce or maple syrup. Serves 4.

FREEZER FRENCH TOAST

Lolita Valcq, Rock Creek Bed & Breakfast
Mile 261 George Parks Highway

"This is a favorite with my bed-and-breakfast guests. I can cater to large groups, so this is great to do the night before."

4 eggs
1 cup milk
1 Tb. sugar
1 tsp. vanilla
1/4 tsp. nutmeg
1/4 tsp. cinnamon
8 slices French bread, 3/4- to 1-inch thick
melted butter

In a medium-size bowl, beat together the eggs, milk, sugar, vanilla, nutmeg and cinnamon. Place bread slices on a rimmed baking sheet. Pour egg mixture over all until the egg mixture is absorbed. Freeze, uncovered, until firm. Package in freezer bags and return to freezer until ready to use. To serve, place desired number of frozen slices on a lightly greased baking sheet. Brush each slice with melted butter and bake in a 400°F oven for 8 minutes. Turn slices over, brush with melted butter, and bake an additional 10 minutes or until nicely browned. Serve topped with powdered sugar, honey or syrup. Serves 4.

SCOTCH TOAST

Gail M. LaRocque, Cinnamon Cache Bakery & Coffee Shop, Mile 72 Klondike Highway South

2 eggs
¹/₂ cup milk
¹/₄ tsp. cinnamon
4 to 6 slices raisin bread
1 to 2 cups quick-cooking rolled oats

Beat eggs, milk and cinnamon together. Dip bread into egg mixture then dredge through rolled oats. Fry until golden brown. Serve with favorite syrup. Serves 2 to 3.

SKILAK OMELET

Chef Greybeard, Alaska Wildland Adventures
Mile 50.1 Sterling Highway

1½ cups fresh, sliced mushrooms
⅓ cup chopped onion
1½ cups fresh asparagus, cut into 1-inch pieces
9 eggs
¼ cup milk
⅛ tsp. pepper
⅓ tsp. garlic salt
1 Tb. chopped fresh parsley (or 1 tsp. dried)
1 Tb. butter or margarine
¾ cup mozzarella, shredded
¼ cup cheddar cheese, shredded

Preheat oven to 325°F. Sauté mushrooms and onion. Set aside and keep warm. Boil or steam the asparagus until hot but still crisp, 2 to 3 minutes. Do not overcook. Set aside and keep warm.

Combine eggs, milk, pepper, garlic salt and parsley, and whip well. Melt butter in an oven-proof, 10-inch nonstick frying pan until melted and beginning to bubble. Pour in egg mixture and cook for 2 to 3 minutes until edges begin to firm. Insert a spatula into the mixture so you can lift the middle of the cooked egg allowing the uncooked to flow under the middle of the omelet.

Cook for 1 minute and lift center again. Begin lifting the edges by sliding a spatula gently under the edges and lifting as you tilt the pan to permit the remaining uncooked egg to flow under the edges into the bottom of the pan. Continue to do this all around the edge, building up the omelet as evenly as possible until the eggs no longer flow. Place the pan on the top rack of the preheated oven for 3 to 4 minutes or until the top of the omelet is cooked but not browned. Remove pan and turn off oven.

Spoon sautéed mushrooms and onions over eggs. Add asparagus. Sprinkle with mozzarella and top with cheddar. Place the pan back in the oven for 2 to 3 minutes to allow cheeses to set.

Using a spatula, loosen the omelet completely, then slide the spatula under the omelet opposite the handle and, as you tip the pan, lift and slide the omelet onto your serving dish. Clean the edges of overcooked egg/cheese. Cut into pie-shaped wedges by chopping downward with the end of a metal spatula. Do not try to slice across omelet or the cheese will stick and pull away. Serves 6.

"Greybeard" is an Alaskan Bush resident, who works as morning chef for Alaska Wildland Adventures Kenai River trips. (Alaska Wildland Adventures operates backcountry lodges on the Kenai and in Denali Park.) He spends his winter months on Caribou Island, Skilak Lake, gathering his winter supply of wood, snowmachining, cross-country skiing, painting with acrylics and dreaming up new recipes.

ALASKAN SOURDOUGH SMOKED YUKON KING SALMON OMELET

Willie and Lovie Johnson
Alaskan Sourdough Bed and Breakfast, Cooper Landing

1/2 cup chopped onion
1/2 cup sliced celery
1/2 cup diced green pepper
1/2 cup sliced mushrooms
3 cups smoked Yukon king salmon, shredded
salt, pepper and Cajun spices to taste
16 eggs, lightly whipped

Sauté onion, celery, green pepper and mushrooms in a large fry pan. Add 1/2 cup of the salmon, and salt, pepper and Cajun spices. Add eggs and cook until almost done. Fold in remainder of salmon and cook for about 2 additional minutes. Serves 8.

EASY GARDEN QUICHE

Theresa Ely, Birch Grove Inn Bed and Breakfast
Fairbanks

1 cup shredded Swiss cheese
1 cup shredded cheddar cheese
1¹/₂ cups chopped vegetables (red peppers, mushrooms,
  yellow summer squash, zucchini)
¹/₂ cup milk
¹/₂ cup whipping cream
6 eggs
¹/₄ tsp. salt
¹/₄ tsp. nutmeg
¹/₈ tsp. pepper

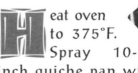

Heat oven to 375°F. Spray 10-inch quiche pan with nonstick spray. Sprinkle cheeses on bottom of prepared pan. Add chopped vegetables. In large bowl, whisk together milk, cream, eggs, salt, nutmeg and pepper. Pour egg mixture over vegetables. Bake for 40 to 45 minutes or until just set in the center. Serves 6.

EASY SPINACH QUICHE

Helen Tucker, Bed & Breakfast On The Park, Anchorage

1 lb. cooked potatoes
olive oil
2 tsp. seasoning salt
8 eggs
2 cups milk
1 package frozen chopped spinach, thawed
1 cup shredded cheddar cheese
1/4 cup parmesan cheese

Slice cooked potatoes into 1/4-inch pieces, and lightly toss with olive oil and 1 tsp. seasoning salt, then place on bottom and sides of quiche pan. Mix eggs, milk and remaining salt together. Squeeze thawed spinach dry and add to eggs. Stir in cheeses and pour mixture over potatoes. Bake for 20 mintes at 375°F, then turn down oven to 350°F and bake until knife inserted in the center comes out clean. Serve warm or at room temperature. Serves 8.

FIREWEED QUICHE

Jeff Watts, Fireweed House Bed & Breakfast, Juneau

6 oz. smoked salmon, skinned and flaked
pie crust
1 cup cooked wild rice
6 oz. grated Gruyere cheese
6 oz. grated Swiss cheese
2 cups cream
1¼ tsp. dry mustard
½ tsp. pepper
½ tsp. dill
3 eggs

Layer salmon on top of unbaked crust, and add wild rice and cheeses. In a separate pan, heat cream, mustard, pepper and dill until scalded. Rapidly beat in eggs and pour into crust. Bake at 375°F for 35 minutes, or until center is no longer jiggly. Remove from oven and let set for a few minutes before cutting. Serves 6 to 8.

SALMON QUICHE

Jolene Schnell
At Schnell's Bed and Breakfast, Anchorage

8 eggs
2 cups cottage cheese
2 tsp. Dijon mustard
pinch of salt
pinch of pepper
1/2 cup finely chopped onion
3/4 lb. smoked salmon, flaked OR 3/4 to 1 lb. fresh broiled
  salmon
1/2 lb. sautéed mushrooms (optional)
prepared pie shell

ix eggs, cottage cheese, mustard, salt, pepper and onion. Add salmon and mushrooms (if desired). Pour into pie shell. Bake at 350°F for 1 to 1 1/4 hours. Serves 6 to 8.

GABLES FRITTATA

Leicha Welton, 7 Gables Inn, Fairbanks

8 oz. sausage
2 cups shredded zucchini
2 green onions, chopped
1/2 tsp. dry basil
1 tsp. Italian seasoning (dressing mix)
6 eggs
1/2 cup half and half OR whipping cream
4 oz. cream cheese, cut in cubes
1 cup each mozzarella and cheddar cheese, shredded

Preheat oven to 325°F. Spray an 8-inch pie plate with non-stick cooking spray. Brown sausage, drain, and place in prepared pan. Spread zucchini and onions over sausage; sprinkle with seasonings. Beat eggs with half and half, and pour over vegetables and sausage. Sprinkle cubed cream cheese, mozarella and cheddar cheese over the top. Bake for 45 minutes or until the middle is set and top is lightly browned. Serves 6.

BREAKFAST TURNOVERS

Carol Kleckner, Birch Haven Inn Bed & Breakfast, Fairbanks

"This is a great recipe to put together the night before. Bake in the morning and serve with fruit garnish and home-fried potatoes."

2 sheets (17-oz. package) frozen puff pastry
4 Tb. finely chopped green onion
2 Tb. butter, melted
2 eggs, beaten
2 cups shredded Swiss cheese
2 cups ham, chopped (vegetarian substitute: mushrooms)
2 tsp. dill
1/2 tsp. garlic powder
1/2 tsp. pepper

Thaw pastry sheet for approximately 30 minutes. Separate sheets and fold each into a 12-inch square. Cut into quarters for a total of 8 squares. In a mixing bowl, combine all other ingredients. Place 1/2-cup of filling in center of each square. Moisten pastry edges with a little water and fold in half, pressing all sides together with a fork. Place on baking sheets. Bake at 400°F for 20 to 25 minutes until golden brown. If prepared the night before, cover baking sheets and refrigerate overnight, then bake as directed in the morning. Serves 8.

EASY EGG SOUFFLÉ

LesLee Solberg, Denali View Bed & Breakfast
Mile 3.1 Talkeetna Spur Road

4 eggs
1 1/2 tsp. salsa
1/3 cup plus 2 heaping tsp. grated cheddar cheese, divided
3/4 cup buttermilk (or less, depending on the density of the eggs)
1 Tb. Bisquick

Preheat oven to 350°F. Mix together eggs, salsa, 1/3 cup cheese, buttermilk and Bisquick. Spray custard cups or small, oven-proof bowls with nonstick cooking spray and pour mixture into bowls, to 3/4-inch from the top of the bowl. Bake in oven for 45 minutes. Top each serving with a heaping teaspoon of cheese. Serves 2.

When increasing recipe, figure 2 eggs per person. Always monitor the buttermilk quantity so that it does not thin the eggs too much; they need to maintain their eggy consistency.

EASY EGG SURPRISE

Helen Tucker, Bed & Breakfast on the Park, Anchorage

10 eggs	**1 tsp.** seasoning salt
1/2 cup grated parmesan cheese	**2 Tb.** medium salsa
(or any cheese you like)	**1 Tb.** butter
1/4 cup milk	**1 lb.** frozen stir-fry vegetables

Mix eggs, cheese, milk, seasoning salt and salsa together; set aside. In hot skillet, add butter and vegetables. Cook until vegetables are thawed and cooked lightly. Add egg mixture and stir until eggs are done. Serve immediately. Serves 6 to 8.

The log "wing" of Bed & Breakfast On The Park was originally a church, built in 1946. The interior of the old church was remodeled in 1992 as guest bedrooms with private baths.

EGGS MARVELOUS

Norine Shandro, Bed & Breakfast Inn Margaree
Dawson Creek

This is a great recipe to make the night before and bake the next morning.

1 cup bacon, ham or sausage
1/4 cup chopped green onion
2 Tb. butter
12 eggs, scrambled,
   soft but not quite set
1 10-oz. can mushrooms, drained
2 cups bread crumbs
3 Tb. melted butter
paprika

Cheese sauce:
2 Tb. butter
2 Tb. flour
2 cups milk
1 1/2 cups old cheese

Sauté bacon, green onions and 2 Tb. butter and set aside. Next make cheese sauce: Melt 2 Tb. butter in saucepan over low heat. Add the flour, and stir for 2 minutes until well incorporated. Turn the heat to medium, and add the milk, stirring constantly until sauce bubbles. Remove from heat, add cheese and stir until melted. Fold eggs, mushrooms, bacon and onion into cheese sauce. Pour into buttered 9" x 12" baking dish. Combine bread crumbs and 3 Tb. melted butter, and pour over mixture. Sprinkle with paprika. Cover and refrigerate overnight. Bake for 40 minutes at 350°F. Serves 8.

FIESTA BRUNCH

Diane Schoming
Morning Glory Bed & Breakfast, Homer

¹/₂ cup **soft butter**
8 slices **firm bread**
2 to 3 cups (¹/₂ to ³/₄ lb.) **grated jack cheese**
1 4-oz. can **diced green chilies**
¹/₂ lb. **bacon, cooked and diced**
6 **eggs**
2 cups **milk**
¹/₂ cup **half and half**
1 tsp. **dry mustard**
¹/₂ tsp. **Tabasco sauce**
1 Tb. **instant minced onions**
¹/₂ tsp. **salt**
salsa

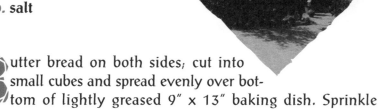

Butter bread on both sides; cut into small cubes and spread evenly over bottom of lightly greased 9" x 13" baking dish. Sprinkle evenly with cheese, diced chilies and bacon.

Combine eggs with milk, half and half, and seasonings. Pour over bread mixture. Cover and refrigerate overnight. Bake uncovered for 45 minutes at 325°F. Serve with salsa, if desired. Serves 8.

HAM AND CHEESE FLORENTINE

Theresa Ely, Birch Grove Inn Bed and Breakfast
Fairbanks

1/2 package **frozen puff-pastry sheet (1 sheet)**
1 **egg, beaten**
1 Tb. **water**
2 **green onions, chopped (about** 1/4 **cup)**
1/2 tsp. **dried oregano leaves, crushed**
1/2 lb. **cooked ham, sliced**
1/2 lb. **cooked turkey, sliced**
1 cup **spinach leaves**
4 oz. **Swiss cheese, sliced**

Thaw pastry at room temperature for 30 minutes. Preheat oven to 400°F. Mix egg and water, and set aside. Mix onions and oregano, and set aside. Unfold pastry on lightly floured surface. Roll into 12" x 16" rectangle. With short side facing you, layer ham, turkey, spinach and cheese on bottom half of pastry to within 1 inch of edge. Sprinkle with onion mixture. Starting at short side, roll into a jelly roll. Place seam side down on baking sheet. Tuck ends under to seal. Brush with egg mixture. Bake 25 minutes or until golden brown. Slice and serve warm. Serves 6.

HEAVENLY FRENCH CUSTARD

Christine & Corbett Upton
Applesauce Inn B&B, Fairbanks

"One guest described this in the guestbook as a 'breakfast to die for,' hence the name."

1 loaf (1 lb.) French baguette bread
light cream cheese
red raspberry jam
8 eggs
3 cups milk (I sometimes use 1 12-oz. can evaporated milk
    and 1 1/2 cups of half and half)
1 Tb. vanilla (clear, if you have it)
1/2 tsp. salt
slivered almonds
butter

Butter a 2-inch-tall, 10-inch casserole dish. Slice bread (minus ends) into 1 1/2-inch slices, making a slit through the middle of the slices, and spread each with cream cheese and 1 Tb. jam. Use enough bread to make one layer in the casserole dish. Whisk eggs, milk, vanilla and salt, then pour mixture over bread. Cover and refrigerate overnight. In the morning, preheat oven to 350°F. Sprinkle slivered almonds on top of casserole and dot with butter. Bake uncovered for 30 to 40 minutes until puffed and golden. Serve with berry and/or maple syrup. Serves 8.

HERBED HAM AND CHEESE BAKE

Christine & Corbett Upton
Applesauce Inn B&B, Fairbanks

"A truly original creation, this casserole is perfectly seasoned by using a high-quality, dense, herbed bread."

1 lb. loaf of dense, herbed bread
8 to 10 slices Canadian bacon
8 to 10 slices white cheese
   (provolone, Swiss or Monterey Jack)
8 large eggs
3 cups milk
1/2 cup grated white cheese

Cut loaf in half lengthwise, trim ends off, then slice crosswise into 8 to 10 pairs of slices, 1-inch thick. Place one slice from each pair into a well-buttered 2-inch-tall by 10-inch casserole dish. Place a slice of Canadian bacon and cheese on each half piece of bread. Cover with other bread halves. Combine eggs and milk, and pour mixture over bread. Refrigerate covered overnight. Uncover and sprinkle with grated cheese. Bake at 350°F for 40 to 50 minutes, until puffed and golden. Serves 6.

McKINLEY BREAKFAST

Leicha Welton, 7 Gables Inn, Fairbanks

²/₃ cup **chopped ham**
²/₃ cup **grated cheddar cheese**
1 Tb. **Dijon mustard**
1 Tb. **mayonnaise**
4 slices **whole wheat bread**
3 **eggs**
1¹/₂ cups **milk**

In medium bowl, combine ham, cheese, mustard and mayonnaise. Make 2 sandwiches using whole wheat bread slices, and ham and cheese mixture. Cut each sandwich diagonally into quarters. Place 2 sandwich triangles each—pointed end up (like mountain peaks)—into 4 oven-proof ramekins sprayed with nonstick cooking spray. In another bowl, combine eggs and milk. Pour equally over the 4 sandwich dishes, making sure the bread has been soaked. Refrigerate overnight and remove about three-quarters of an hour before baking. Bake in preheated 325°F oven for 30 minutes. Serves 4.

MY DAD'S BAKED EGGS

Ronald S. Pendleton, Journeymen's B&B, Homer

butter
7 slices processed cheese
6 eggs
milk OR cream
garlic salt

Line a baking dish with butter. Put 6 slices of cheese on bottom of dish and crack eggs onto cheese. Pour a dot of milk or cream on each yolk. Crumble the other slice of cheese on top of the eggs, and season with garlic salt. Bake at 400°F for about 10 minutes, or until set. Serve with cornmeal muffins.

NORTH COUNTRY GLACIER MELTER

Cindy H. Kinard, North Country Castle Bed & Breakfast
Anchorage

12 slices wheat bread
6 Tb. butter
11 Tb. grated parmesan cheese, divided
1 7-oz. can diced mild chilies
1/2 tsp. diced jalapeño peppers
6 artichoke hearts (canned), chopped
4 large eggs, beaten 'til creamy yellow
21/4 cup milk
6 tsp. diced pimiento

Trim crusts from bread. Melt butter in microwave in a 9" x 13" casserole dish. Dip one side of 6 bread slices in the butter to cover lightly; set aside. Place remaining 6 slices in remaining butter in casserole. Top bread with mixture of 5 Tb. cheese, mild chilies, jalapeño peppers and artichokes. Place set-aside bread slices over cheese mixture, butter side up. Mix eggs and milk, and pour over bread stacks. Top each bread stack with 1 tsp. pimiento and 1 Tb. parmesan cheese. Cover and refrigerate 1 hour or overnight. Bake uncovered in preheated, 350°F oven for 45 minutes, or until knife inserted in center comes out clean. Serves 6.

SAUSAGE STRATA ELEANOR

La Verne Wood, Eleanor's Northern Lights Bed & Breakfast, Fairbanks

This is a good old standard. It is particularly good because it can be prepared the night before serving.

4 Tb. butter
8 slices white bread, trimmed and quartered
1 lb. cheddar cheese (mild to sharp), shredded
1 lb. breakfast sausage, fried and diced
2 cups milk
4 eggs
1 20-oz. can cream of mushroom soup
1/2 tsp. dry mustard
1/2 tsp. salt
1 small can sliced mushrooms, or sautéed fresh mushrooms

Layer the bread, cheese and sausage in a buttered 9" x 12" baking dish. You should get at least 2 layers. Mix milk, eggs, soup, mustard and salt, and pour over layers. Cover and let sit overnight in the refrigerator. Before baking, spread mushrooms on top. Bake at 350°F for approximately 1 hour. Check with knife for doneness: knife should be dry. Let cool 10 minutes before cutting. Serves 8 to 10.

CHOCOLATE DROP B&B'S SAUSAGE STRATA

Judy Ceglie, Chocolate Drop B&B, Homer

7 slices **bread**
2 lbs. **sausage**
1 small can **sliced mushrooms, drained**
9 **eggs**
1 pint **half and half**
1/4 tsp. **salt**
3/4 tsp. **dry mustard**
2 Tb. **onion flakes**
2 cups **shredded sharp cheddar cheese**

Butter a 9" x 13" baking dish, and place bread on bottom of dish. Cook sausage, crumbling while stirring. Drain and place over bread. Layer mushrooms over sausage. Beat eggs, add cream, and then spices and onion flakes. Pour over sausage. Sprinkle cheese over top. Refrigerate overnight, if desired. Bake at 375°F for 45 minutes until brown and bubbly. Serves 12 to 15.

SAUSAGE-CHEESE BREAKFAST STRATA

Betty Heinrichs, Wintel's Bed and Breakfast, Kodiak

10 cups **cubed French bread (1/2- to 3/4-inch pieces)**
3/4 cup **fully cooked smoked sausage links, cut into 3/4-inch pieces**
1 4-oz. can **mushroom stems and pieces, drained**
1 1/2 cups **shredded sharp cheddar cheese**
1 cup **shredded Monterey Jack cheese with jalapeño peppers**
7 **eggs, beaten**
3 1/2 cups **milk**
2 Tb. **snipped fresh chives**
1 Tb. **vinegar**
1/2 tsp. **salt**
1/4 tsp. **pepper**
1/2 tsp. **seasoned salt**
2 tsp. **dried marjoram, crushed**
1 tsp. **dry mustard**

In two 2-quart, greased casseroles, put one half of bread cubes, sausage and mushrooms. Sprinkle with cheese. Top with remaining bread, sauage and mushrooms. Combine eggs, milk, chives, vinegar and seasonings. Divide evenly and pour over casseroles. Cover and refrigerate a minimum of 2 hours, or up to 48 hours. Bake uncovered at 325°F for 1 hour. Serves 12.

Appetizers

The remains of Montague House, a typical early-day road-house, can be seen along the Klondike Highway, approximately 89 miles north of Whitehorse, Yukon Territory. A total of 52 stopping places on the winter trail between Whitehorse and Dawson City, offering lodging and meals to travelers, were listed in the Jan. 16, 1901, edition of the "Whitehorse Star." Montague House was listed at Mile 99 along the stagecoach route.

Appetizers

SWISS CHEESE FONDUE

Hap Wurlitzer, Hatcher Pass Lodge
Mile 17.5 Fishhook-Willow Road

1/2 loaf French bread
1/2 apple, sliced
1 clove garlic
2 shots white wine
1 shot cherry brandy (kirsch)
5 oz. grated Swiss Gruyere cheese
5 oz. grated Swiss Emmentaler cheese
dash black pepper
dash nutmeg
1 tsp. lemon juice

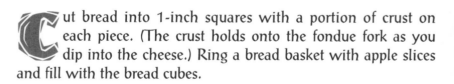

Cut bread into 1-inch squares with a portion of crust on each piece. (The crust holds onto the fondue fork as you dip into the cheese.) Ring a bread basket with apple slices and fill with the bread cubes.

Rub the fondue pan with the garlic clove, until it is crushed. Put in the shots of wine and brandy. Over a low heat, add the grated cheeses. With the end of a wooden spoon stir in a figure-8 pattern until the cheese is well-melted and of a smooth consistency. Add the pepper, nutmeg and lemon juice, continuing to mix into a smooth cheese. Serves 2 to 4.

CRAB-STUFFED MUSHROOMS

Deb Kremzar, Bitter Creek Cafe & Mercantile, Stewart

1/4 cup butter
4 Tb. minced onion
1 large clove garlic, crushed
3 Tb. flour
1/2 to 3/4 cup milk
1 Tb. fresh dill (or 1 tsp. dried)
2 Tb. fresh lemon juice
salt and pepper to taste
1 to 1 1/2 cups crab meat
12 to 16 white mushroom caps
grated parmesan cheese
garlic butter to taste

Melt butter in saucepan; add onion and garlic, and sauté. Add flour and cook over medium-low heat for 2 minutes. Add milk gradually, until you reach a fairly thick consistency. Add dill, lemon juice, salt and pepper. Add enough crab meat to sauce to hold it together. Stuff mushroom caps with crab mixture and sprinkle with grated parmesan cheese. Broil in garlic butter for 15 minutes or until mushrooms are cooked. Serves 6 to 8.

Appetizers

DEEP-FRIED FIDDLEHEADS IN BEER BATTER

Mary Carey, Mary's McKinley View Lodge
Mile 134.5 George Parks Highway

"At Mary's McKinley View Lodge, I became noted for food that is different. Patrons often drove to my place all the way from Anchorage, and from towns and villages along the route, to eat my fiddlehead fern specialties.

"I became interested in working with ferns after homesteading in a fly-in area. For me the nearest supermarket was over a hundred miles away. Fresh greens were, and still are, a precious commodity."

1 qt. fresh fiddleheads, 3-inch necks
1 cup flour
2 tsp. salt
1 tsp. pepper

Batter:
4 egg whites
1 bottle beer
1 cup flour

If fern is not completely dry, blot dry with paper towels. Put dry mixture into paper bag and shake a little of the fern at a time, as you would chicken.

For batter, beat egg whites until stiff. Add beer and flour. Whip until stiff. Dip fiddleheads into batter by holding tips of stems.

Deep fry until golden brown. (Excerpted with permission from "Let's Taste Alaska.")

Mary Carey has been extolling the virtues of the fiddlehead fern, in particular the ostrich fern (Matteuccia struthiopteris), since she was first introduced to the green while teaching school in Talkeetna in 1962. She also has the world's only fiddlehead fern farm (see photo below), located on the Talkeetna Spur Road. Fiddleheads are picked in early spring when the tightly coiled clusters resemble a fiddle's head. The ostrich fern is a favorite because of its flavor and because it has the least amount of flaky brown coating, which must be picked off before use. The ostrich fern is also distinguished by a central fertile frond that is surrounded by taller, green, sterile fronds. Fiddleheads should be served cooked.

BOURSIN AU POIVRE

Lynn Coutts, The Noland House, Atlin

1 8-oz. package cream cheese, room temperature
1 clove garlic, crushed
1 tsp. dill
1 tsp. caraway seeds
1 tsp. basil
1 tsp. chives, chopped
Lemon pepper to taste

Blend cheese with all ingredients except lemon pepper. Pat into round, flattened shape between two layers of wax paper. Roll on all sides in lemon pepper. Refrigerate, covered. Keeps well for several days. Serve with bagels, crackers, etc. Serves 8.

TURNAGAIN HOUSE MUSHROOMS

Turnagain House, Mile 103.1 Seward Highway

4 oz. chopped scallops
4 oz. chopped shrimp
1/2 lb. chopped mushroom stems
4 green onions, chopped
1 tsp. fresh tarragon
3 oz. white wine
1 oz. brandy
juice from 1/2 lemon

18 large mushroom caps
2 to 3 Tb. butter
salt
pepper
cayenne
3/4 lb. cream cheese
grated parmesan cheese
bread crumbs

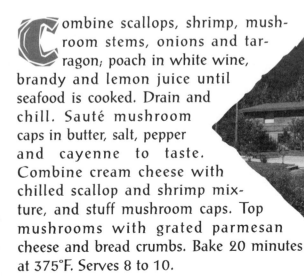

Combine scallops, shrimp, mushroom stems, onions and tarragon; poach in white wine, brandy and lemon juice until seafood is cooked. Drain and chill. Sauté mushroom caps in butter, salt, pepper and cayenne to taste. Combine cream cheese with chilled scallop and shrimp mixture, and stuff mushroom caps. Top mushrooms with grated parmesan cheese and bread crumbs. Bake 20 minutes at 375°F. Serves 8 to 10.

GUEST HOUSE SPECIAL

Red Salmon Guest House, Mile 48.2 Sterling Highway

Herbed cream cheese:
1/2 tsp. chopped chives
1 1/2 tsp. chopped parsley
2 tsp. chopped whole
   green onion
1 small garlic clove, peeled
3/4 tsp. tarragon vinegar
2 dashes fresh, finely
   ground pepper
6 2/3 oz. cream cheese

4 bagels, halved and toasted
4 dabs herbed cream cheese
4 handfuls smoked salmon,
   crumbled
1 lemon
parsley

Place all the ingredients for herbed cream cheese, except the cream cheese, into the bowl of a good food processor fitted with a steel S-blade. Process for 15 seconds. In a separate mixing bowl, combine the herb mixture and cream cheese, and beat thoroughly with an electric mixer. Herbed cream cheese can be refrigerated up to a week. (Note: If desired, reserve a tablespoon of the herb mixture and mix with 1/2 cup mayonnaise to use on sandwiches or hamburgers.)

Spread herbed cream cheese on toasted bagels. Sprinkle each bagel half with salmon; squeeze a bit of lemon juice on top; and sprinkle with chopped parsley. Garnish with lemon slices and sprigs of parsley. Serves 4.

Beverages

Described as the "farthest north of the old-time Richardson trail hostelries," the ruins of the old Black Rapids Hunting Lodge may be seen at Mile V 227.4 Richardson Highway. The Richardson Highway began as a trail for gold stampeders in 1898 and became Alaska's first road—connecting Fairbanks with Valdez—when it was updated to automobile standards in the 1920s. A number of roadhouses that served the early traffic along the Richardson still exist, including Tsaina Lodge, Tiekel River Lodge, Tonsina Lodge, Copper Center Lodge and Paxson Lodge.

CRANBERRY MINT PUNCH

Mary Carey, Mary's McKinley View Lodge
Mile 134.5 Parks Highway

4 cups **lowbush cranberry juice**
4 cups **water**
2 cups **pineapple juice**
2 cups **orange juice**
1/2 cup **sugar**
1/2 cup **mint sprigs**
1 **orange, thinly sliced**

Combine all ingredients except orange slices and mint. Mix well. Serve over ice. Garnish with a sprig of mint and orange slice. Prettier if orange slice is split to the center and hung over edge of glass. (Excerpted with permission from "Let's Taste Alaska.")

Octogenarian Mary Carey is an Alaska homesteader, author of 12 books, and runs not only the McKinley View Lodge but also the "world's only fiddlehead fern farm", located a mile off the Talkeetna Spur Road. Mary came to Alaska in 1963, and taught school in Talkeetna. She has also worked as a reporter, and had a weekly newspaper column.

RASPBERRY-RHUBARB SPICED PUNCH

Mary Carey, Mary's McKinley View Lodge
Mile 134.5 Parks Highway

4 **cups** raspberries
4 **cups** thinly sliced rhubarb
1 **cup** sugar
3 **sticks** cinnamon
12 **whole** cloves
1 **tsp.** nutmeg
1 **lemon**, sliced
4 **cups** freshly brewed tea

Cook berries and rhubarb 3 minutes in just enough water to cover. Put through colander. Strain through cheesecloth into tea. Tie spices in cheesecloth and boil in tea for 5 minutes. Serve hot with dash of nutmeg and a lemon slice. (Excerpted with permission from "Let's Taste Alaska.")

MULLED WINE

Sharon Waisanen, Spruce Avenue Bed & Breakfast
Kenai Spur Highway

"We serve this to guests during the holidays or for ourselves on a blustery, snowy Alaskan night."

1 cup **sugar**
2 to 3 **sticks cinnamon**
12 **whole allspice**
1 cup **water**
12 **whole cloves**
1 **lemon**
3 cups **red wine**

immer everything but wine for 5 minutes. Let stand 30 minutes. Add wine, heat until just under boiling.

ORANGE JUICE SPECIAL

Rose Ringstad, Rose's Forget-Me-Not B&B, Fairbanks

1/2 16-oz. package frozen strawberries
1 12-oz. can frozen orange juice

Cut 16-oz. package of frozen strawberries in half length-wise, then chop one of the halves into 8 pieces. Combine concentrated orange juice and frozen strawberries in blender and add water to fill blender. Blend at medium speed for 30 to 40 seconds. Stir and serve while still frosty and frothy, topping each glass with a fresh strawberry. Serves 6.

Breads

anley Roadhouse, in Manley Hot Springs at Mile 152 Elliott Highway, has been serving Alaska since 1906. One of Alaska's oldest original roadhouses, the Manley Roadhouse offers "traditional Alaska home-style hospitality" and "good food." It is located on Manley Slough in a field of irises. It is a community gathering place for local miners, trappers, dog mushers and fishermen. The roadhouse has some wonderful prehistoric fossils on display that were unearthed by miners.

ALASKA BACKPACK MOUNTAIN BREAD

Jan Thacker
Coldfoot Services and Arctic Acres Inn, Coldfoot

"This bread will keep for 3 weeks. It is almost a meal and very high in energy."

4 cups whole wheat flour
1 cup water
3/4 cup brown sugar
1/2 cup honey
1/3 cup wheat germ
1/3 cup vegetable oil
1/4 cup sesame seed
1/4 cup molasses
3 Tb. dry milk powder
11/2 tsp. salt
11/2 tsp. baking soda

ix all ingredients until smooth. Pour into greased 8" x 8" x 2" pan. Bake at 300°F for about 1 hour, or until bread pulls away from sides of pan. Cool and cut into 16 equal squares. Makes 1 loaf.

"NUTS ABOUT BANANA" BREAD

Christine and Corbett Upton
Cedar Creek Inn, Fairbanks

"I was not a banana bread fan until I found this recipe. Even though Cedar Creek Inn vacation home guests do their own cooking, I often send over a loaf with their breakfast stock."

1 cup **sugar**
1 Tb. **molasses**
¹/₂ cup **vegetable oil**
2 **eggs**
1 Tb. **plain yogurt**
3 **bananas, mashed**
1 tsp. **lemon juice**
2 tsp. **baking powder**
¹/₄ tsp. **salt**
2 cups **flour**
¹/₂ tsp. **baking soda**
1 cup **coarse nuts**

ix well the first 9 ingredients. Add flour, baking soda and lastly the nuts. Pour batter into greased loaf pan. Bake 1 hour at 375°F, until loaf tests done.

LAKE HOUSE BED & BREAKFAST BUBBLE BREAD

Marilyn Talmage, Lake House Bed & Breakfast, Valdez

2 packages **active dry yeast**
1 cup **granulated sugar**
1/2 cup **warm water (100° to 115°F)**
2 sticks (1 cup) **softened sweet butter or margarine**
1 1/2 Tb. **salt**
1 cup **warm milk**
3 **eggs,** plus 2 **egg yolks**
6 to 7 cups **all-purpose flour**
1/2 cup **brown sugar**
1/2 cup **dried cranberries, dried cherries or raisins**

ombine the yeast, white sugar and water in a large mixing bowl. While this is proofing, stir 1 stick of the butter and the salt into the warm milk. Add to the yeast mixture. Stir in all the eggs. Beat with a wooden spoon to blend thoroughly. Add the flour, 1 cup at a time, stirring well after each addition. Turn dough out on a floured board and knead, adding more flour as needed until the dough is no longer sticky. Knead a full 10 minutes, until the dough is elastic and pliable. Shape into a ball and put in a buttered bowl, turning to coat all over with butter. Cover with plastic wrap and set in a warm, draft-free place to rise until doubled in bulk. Punch the dough down and let rest for 5

minutes. Turn out on a lightly floured board and again shape into a ball. Let rest for another 5 to 10 minutes. While the dough is resting, butter a 10-inch tube pan.

In a saucepan, melt the second stick of sweet butter with the brown sugar and cranberries. Pinch off enough dough to make golf ball-sized balls. Roll the balls in the butter mixture and place in bottom of the tube pan arranging balls in loose layers. Pour what is left of the butter mixture over the top. Cover loosely with a foil tent and let the dough rise to the top of the tube pan. Bake in a preheated 375°F oven for about 1 hour. When bread is ready, the top will sound hollow when tapped. Unmold and let cool thoroughly before slicing, or serve warm and pull apart. Yields 1 ring loaf.

SHIRLEY'S HERB FOCCACIA

M.M. Clay, Sportsman's Kispiox Lodge, Hazelton

3 tsp. yeast
1/2 tsp. sugar
21/2 cups warm water, divided
11/2 cups milk OR sour milk
1 tsp. salt
1/2 cup oil
1 tsp. oregano
1/2 cup parmesan cheese
7 cups flour

Dissolve yeast and sugar in 1/2 cup warm water. Mix together 2 cups warm water, milk, salt, oil, oregano, parmesan cheese, flour and the dissolved yeast mixture. Knead. Let rise in bowl for 1/2 hour; punch down, divide into 4 parts and put in 4 greased, round cake pans. Let rise for 1/2 hour. Dimple the surface with your fingertips and sprinkle with coarse salt. Bake in 350°F oven for 1/2 hour.

SOURDOUGH FRENCH BREAD

Gail Corbin, Lisianski Inlet Lodge, Pelican

1¹/₂ cups **sourdough starter**
1¹/₂ cups **warm water**
1 Tb. **sugar**
1 Tb. **yeast**
2 tsp. **salt**
5 cups **flour**
¹/₂ tsp. **baking soda**

Mix in large bowl sourdough starter, water, sugar, yeast and salt. Let it set to dissolve yeast for 3 minutes. Add 3 or more cups of flour to make a thick batter. Raise until double in bulk. Add 1 cup flour with baking soda. Turn out and knead. Cut into 2 balls. Rest for 10 minutes. Shape into long, skinny loaves on cookie sheet buttered and coated with corn meal. Slash across top. Raise. Bake at 425°F for 15 minutes. Brush with salted water. Bake at 375°F for 20 to 30 minutes, or until done (sounds hollow when tapped on bottom). Makes 2 loaves.

TWO-TONE BREAD

Camp Denali and North Face Lodge, Denali National Park

"In this popular dinner bread, two colors of dough form an attractive spiral."

3 cups **lukewarm water**
1/2 cup **honey**
2 Tb. **active dry yeast**
31/2 cups **unbleached white flour**
1/2 cup **nonfat powdered milk**
1/2 cup **vegetable oil**
2 tsp. **salt**
1/2 cup **bran**
2 cups **unbleached white flour**
1/4 cup **molasses**
2 Tb. **instant coffee granules**
21/2 cups **whole wheat flour**
1 cup **unbleached white flour**

Mix together water and honey; add yeast. When yeast mixture is foamy, add 31/2 cups white flour, powdered milk, vegetable oil and salt. Stir vigorously, about 200 strokes. Divide dough in half. To one half gradually stir in bran and 2 cups white flour. To the other half, stir in molasses, coffee granules, wheat flour and 1 cup white flour. Knead each half separately, adding additional white flour as necessary until doughs are smooth and elastic. Place doughs in separate oiled bowls,

cover and let rise in a warm place until doubled in bulk. Punch down and divide each dough in half.

Roll out one piece of light dough into an 8" x 12" rectangle. Repeat with a piece of dark dough. Place one colored dough atop the other and roll out together into a larger rectangle, about 10" x 15", taking care to press out any air bubbles between layers. Roll up from the short side. Pinch seams together and place seam-side-down in a greased loaf pan. Repeat process with the two remaining pieces of dough. Cover and let rise in a warm place until almost doubled. Bake at 350°F for 40 to 45 minutes. Makes 2 5" x 9" loaves.

Founded in 1951, Camp Denali was one of Denali National Park's first wilderness vacation lodges. It is also a nature center, specializing in natural history and guided hiking activities, with special programs on Northern studies. The rustic, hand-crafted cabins cluster around a centralized dining room lodge. Camp Denali is located about a mile from North Face Lodge.

SOURDOUGH PAUL'S BANANA NUT BREAD

Paul Miebs, Sourdough Paul's Bed and Breakfast
Mile 193 George Parks Highway

See Paul's sourdough starter method on opposite page. No sourdough sponge is necessary for this recipe.

1 cup **sugar**
1/3 cup **vegetable oil**
2 eggs, **beaten**
1/2 cup **sourdough starter**
2 cups **all-purpose flour**
1 tsp. **salt**
1 tsp. **baking soda**
3 **ripe bananas, mashed**
2/3 cup **chopped walnuts**

Mix sugar and oil together. Beat in the eggs. Gently fold in the sourdough starter. Add together all the remaining ingredients. Preheat oven to 375°F. Bake in greased and floured bread pan in the center of oven for 40 to 50 minutes or until inserted toothpick comes out clean. Cool on rack.

Starter:
3 medium potatoes, peeled and cut into pieces
3 cups water
1 package active yeast
1¹/₂ Tb. sugar, divided
2 cups flour, all-purpose unbleached preferred

Boil potatoes in water until soft. Save the potato water for the starter; use the potatoes for dinner. Pour just 2 cups potato water into a glass bowl. Let cool until lukewarm. Mix the yeast and ¹/₂ Tb. sugar into potato water. Let stand until yeast is working (light and frothy looking). Add 2 cups flour and 1 Tb. sugar, and then mix it up good. Now cover bowl with towel, and let it set in a warm place for 3 days or more, until it is really bubbly looking. Be sure to stir the starter mixture each day. After 3 days, your new starter is ready for use in recipes.

Never store your starter in a plastic or metal container! Always use glass or pottery. Store starter in a cool place; the refrigerator if you have the luxury. Don't tightly seal your starter, as it needs air to breathe and grow. Sprinkle a little sugar on top to aid in the fermenting process when storing. If the water starts to separate in your starter, don't pour it off, just mix it back in and keep in a cool place. If a crust begins to appear on the surface, don't worry, just set it out at room temperature, and it will dissolve back into itself. Do not get salt into the starter at any cost. Salt kills sourdough! Do not use self-rising flour. Be sure to use your starter at least once every 2 weeks or more. Key secret: Use it or lose it.

ALASKA CRANBERRY MUFFINS

Pat Dwinnell, Longmere Lake Lodge B&B, Soldotna

"I have been serving these to our family and friends for the past 20-plus years we have lived in Alaska. Since opening our lodge, I now serve them to our guests, and everyone likes them."

1¼ cups **flour**
½ cup **sugar**
1 Tb. **baking powder**
¼ tsp. **salt**
1 Tb. **grated, dried orange peel**
2 cups **all-bran cereal**
1¼ cups **milk**
1 **egg**
¼ cup **vegetable oil**
1 cup **lowbush cranberries**

ift together flour, sugar, baking powder, salt and orange peel, and set aside. In a large bowl, combine cereal, milk, egg and oil. Let it set for 5 minutes and then beat together. Add flour mixture, stirring only until combined. Add lowbush cranberries, dusted with 1 Tb. flour, and fold into the batter without breaking open the berries. I add them right from the freezer. Pour batter into muffin tins that have been sprayed with nonstick spray. Bake at 400°F for about 20 minutes. Makes 12 large muffins.

CRAISIN PUFFIN MUFFINS

Sandy Schroth, A Puffin's Bed & Breakfast, Gustavus

2 cups all-bran cereal
1 cup milk
1/4 cup oil, melted butter or margarine
1 egg, beaten
1/4 cup crushed pineapple, not drained
1/3 cup dried cranberries
1/4 cup sugar
11/4 cups all-purpose flour
1 Tb. baking powder
1/4 tsp. salt
1/4 tsp. cinnamon (optional)

Combine cereal and milk in a small bowl, and let stand for 5 minutes. Add oil, egg, pineapple and dried cranberries, and set aside. In a large bowl, combine sugar, flour, baking powder, salt and cinnamon. Add ingredients from the small bowl to the ingredients in the large bowl. Mix only until moistened. Add a little more pineapple juice if the batter looks too dry. Grease muffin tins, or use paper wrappers. Fill muffin tins 2/3 full. Bake at 400°F for 15 minutes or until lightly browned. Makes 16 muffins.

CRANBERRY BANANA BREAD/MUFFINS

Geraldine Jauhola, Finnish Alaskan Bed & Breakfast
Mile 302.1 George Parks Highway

³/₄ cup **fresh or frozen cranberries, chopped**
1 cup **sugar, divided in half**
1 tsp. **grated orange peel**

1³/₄ **cups flour**	2 **eggs**
2 tsp. **baking powder**	³/₄ cup **mashed banana (2 small)**
¹/₂ tsp. **baking soda**	¹/₃ cup **vegetable oil**
¹/₂ tsp. **salt**	¹/₂ cup **chopped walnuts**

In a small mixing bowl, combine cranberries, ¹/₂ cup of the sugar, and orange peel. Set aside. In large mixing bowl, sift together flour, remaining ¹/₂ cup of sugar, baking powder, baking soda and salt. In medium mixing bowl, combine eggs, bananas and oil; stir well with fork to combine. Add banana mixture to dry ingredients, stirring just enough to moisten. Stir in cranberry mixture and walnuts. Pour into well-greased and floured or parchment-lined 9" x 5" x 3" loaf pan, or lined muffin pan. Bake in preheated 350°F oven for 1 hour (bread) or 16 to 20 minutes (muffins). Done when golden brown and toothpick inserted in center comes out clean. Remove from pan and cool on rack. Serves 6.

GREEN APPLE MUFFINS

Ed & Dana Klinkhart
Snowline Bed & Breakfast, Anchorage

2 cups **sugar**
1¹/₂ cups **vegetable oil**
3 **eggs, beaten**
2 tsp. **vanilla**
3 cups **flour**
1 tsp. **baking soda**
1 tsp. **salt**
3 cups **grated, unpeeled green apples (2 large)**
1 cup **chopped walnuts**

In a large mixing bowl, mix together sugar and oil. Add beaten eggs and vanilla. Stir in dry ingredients. Mixture will be thick. Fold in grated apples and nuts. Blend well. Pour into lined muffin tin. Bake at 350° for 20 to 25 minutes for regular muffins, or for 35 to 40 minutes for extra large "mega" muffins. Check with a toothpick for doneness. Makes 12 to 14 mega muffins.

HEARTSTONE MUFFINS

Jan Guertin, Jan's View Bed & Breakfast, Juneau

"This recipe makes a gallon of batter, and it will keep in the refrigerator for up to 6 weeks. Just use as needed."

5 cups sifted flour
3 cups sugar
12 oz. raisin bran cereal
5 tsp. baking soda
2 tsp. salt
1 tsp. cinnamon
1/2 tsp. allspice
4 beaten eggs
1 qt. buttermilk
1 cup oil

Preheat oven to 350°F. Mix dry ingredients together. Add eggs, buttermilk and oil. Fill greased muffin tins ²/₃ full. Bake 15 minutes or until golden brown. Makes 6 to 7 dozen.

MARVELOUS MUFFINS

Leicha Welton, 7 Gables Inn, Fairbanks

1/2 cup **sugar**
1/3 cup **orange juice**
1/2 cup **butter**
1 cup **sugar**
1/2 cup **oil**
11/2 cups **plain yogurt**
4 cups **flour**
2 tsp. **baking soda**
2 tsp. **salt**
2 tsp. **grated orange peel**
1 cup **raisins**
1 cup **chopped walnuts**

Combine 1/2 cup sugar and orange juice; set aside for topping. Cream butter, 1 cup ugar and oil, then blend in the yogurt. Combine dry ingredients and add them to the creamed mixture, stirring just until the ingredients are combined. Stir in grated orange peel, raisins and nuts. The batter will be stiff. Place in muffin tins, filling cups 3/4 full. Bake at 350°F for 15 minutes. While warm, dip top of each muffin into sugar-orange juice mixture. Makes 2 dozen muffins.

MIDNIGHT SUN MUFFINS
Gail M. LaRocque
Cinnamon Cache Bakery & Coffee Shop, Carcross

"I use applesauce instead of oil to make low-fat muffins."

2 cups **whole wheat flour**
1 cup **sugar**
2 tsp. **baking soda**
2 cups **grated carrots OR apples**
1/3 cup **chopped dry apricots**
1/3 cup **sunflower seeds**
1/3 cup **raisins**
1 **banana, mashed**
3 **eggs**
1 cup **oil OR applesauce**
2 tsp. **vanilla**

Combine dry ingredients and mix well. Stir in fruit and nuts. Beat together eggs, oil and vanilla. Stir into flour mixture until moistened. Spoon into muffin tins, and bake at 375°F for 15 to 20 minutes. Makes 15 large muffins.

MOM'S MUFFINS

Reva Jurgeleit, Cedarvale Cafe, Yellowhead Highway 16

6 eggs
1 cup sugar
1 cup walnuts
1 cup raisins
1 cup grated carrot
1¹/₃ cups vegetable oil
1 can crushed pineapple
1 Tb. cinnamon
2 cups bran
4 cups flour
4 tsp. baking powder
1 tsp. baking soda

Beat eggs and sugar well. Add walnuts, raisins and grated carrot; mix well. Add oil, pineapple and cinnamon; mix well. Add bran and flour; mix well. Add baking powder and baking soda; mix well. Pour evenly into 2 muffin tins. Bake at 375°F for 35 minutes. Makes 2 dozen.

PUMPKIN MUFFINS

Susan and Ken Risse
The Blue Goose Bed & Breakfast, Fairbanks

"Every fall I freeze a bunch of pumpkin. I cut the pumpkin in pieces, and bake at 350°F until a fork goes in easily. I then cut away the skin and purée the pumpkin in the food processor with the steel blade. Measure 1 cup, put in a small plastic bag and freeze. This is one of my most asked-for recipes, and the thing that makes it is the fresh frozen pumpkin."

1 cup **mashed pumpkin (fresh frozen)**	1 tsp. **baking soda**
1/2 cup **oil**	1/4 tsp. **nutmeg**
1/4 cup **water**	1/4 tsp. **cinnamon**
2 **eggs**	1/4 tsp. **allspice**
1 cup **sugar**	1/2 cup **berries**
1 1/2 cups **flour**	1/2 cup **chopped nuts**
1/2 tsp. **salt**	

Mix pumpkin, oil, water, eggs and sugar in one bowl. Mix flour, salt, baking soda, nutmeg, cinnamon and allspice in another bowl. Combine two mixtures. Add berries and nuts. Pour batter into muffin tins and sprinkle fairly heavily with cinnamon sugar. Bake at 350°F for 25 minutes. Makes 12 muffins.

SOURDOUGH BLUEBERRY MUFFINS

Carla Pitzel
Hawkins House Bed and Breakfast, Whitehorse

Set the sponge at least 6 to 8 hours before making these muffins (see Sourdough Starter recipe on page 86 for sponge directions).

1¹/₂ cups **whole-wheat flour**
¹/₂ cup **sugar**
1 tsp. **salt**
¹/₄ cup **nonfat dry milk**
1 **egg**
¹/₂ cup **melted butter or vegetable oil**
Sourdough sponge
³/₄ cup **blueberries**
1 tsp. **baking soda**
1 Tb. **water**

Sift flour, sugar, salt and nonfat dry milk into a bowl. Make a well in the center. Mix egg and butter thoroughly into sponge. Add this to the well in the flour. Stir only enough to moisten the flour mixture. Add blueberries. Dissolve soda in water. Add this mixture to the batter just before filling the muffin tins. Fill greased muffin tins ³/₄ full. Bake in 375°F oven for 30 to 35 minutes. Yields 20 small or 12 large muffins.

SOURDOUGH STARTER AND SPONGE

Carla Pitzel, Hawkins House Bed and Breakfast, Whitehorse

"Sourdough isn't for a beginner cook, but it's a fun challenge for an experienced one. This yeast-based starter makes it easier. If you want to make a real starter, omit the yeast and add 4 Tb. sugar and 1¹/₂ tsp. salt to the start and it will sour the same, only it takes about 5 days. If you make it this way, you will need fresh-ground, organic flour and pure water (which hasn't been chlorinated or treated), otherwise it may not work."

Sourdough Starter:
2 cups flour
1 tsp. salt
3 Tb. sugar
¹/₂ tsp. yeast
2 cups warm water

Take a gallon crock and add all ingredients. Stir mixture until it is a smooth, thin paste. Cover with lid and set in a warm place on the kitchen counter to sour. Stir it several times a day. In 2 or 3 days your sourdough will be ready. This is your Sourdough Starter. Now you are ready to make your Sponge. (Your starter will keep indefinitely in a clean, covered glass container in the refrigerator. Never use a metal container or leave a metal spoon in the starter or sponge. If unused for several weeks, the starter may need to sit out an extra night before adding the flour and water for the sponge.)

Sourdough Sponge:
2 cups flour
1 Tb. sugar
1/2 tsp. salt
2 cups water

ake the sponge the night before you want to make your muffins. Add all ingredients to the starter and beat well. Set in a warm place, free from draft, to develop overnight. In the moning, the sponge will have gained half again its bulk and will be covered with air bubbles. It will have a pleasant yeasty odor.

HOMEMADE BUNS

Harmke DeBruin, Spirit Lake Wilderness Resort
Mile 72.3 Klondike Highway

16 cups flour
4 Tb. yeast
4 eggs
6 Tb. sugar
12 Tb. oil
6 cups lukewarm water
salt to taste

In a large bowl mix 12 cups flour and yeast. In another bowl mix eggs, sugar, oil, water and salt. Combine together using a wooden spoon. Add the other 4 cups of flour to the mixture. The dough is right when it doesn't stick to your hands anymore. Cover the dough with a towel and let it rise in a warm place for 30 minutes. Punch it down with your fingers and let it rise for another 30 minutes. Put the dough in pans (you can make either buns or loaves) and let it rise another hour. Let it bake for 20 to 25 minutes at 350°F. If you want low-calorie buns, then don't use the sugar. Makes large 25 buns.

ORANGE RYE ROLLS

Camp Denali and North Face Lodge
Denali National Park

1¹/₄ cups **lukewarm water**
¹/₃ cup **molasses**
2 Tb. **honey**
2 Tb. **active dry yeast**
³/₄ cup **orange juice concentrate**
1 Tb. **finely grated orange rind**
1¹/₂ cups **rye flour**

1¹/₂ cups **whole-wheat flour**
¹/₂ cup **vegetable oil**
3 **eggs**
³/₄ tsp. **baking soda**
1 tsp. **salt**
3 cups **unbleached white flour (approximately)**

Mix together water, molasses and honey. Add yeast. When yeast mixture is foamy, add orange juice concentrate, orange rind, rye flour, whole wheat flour, vegetable oil, 2 of the eggs, baking soda and salt. Stir vigorously, about 200 strokes. Gradually stir in enough white flour to form a soft dough. Knead until smooth. Place in an oiled bowl, cover and let rise in a warm place until doubled in bulk. Punch down and shape into rolls. Place on a greased baking sheet, about ¹/₂ inch apart. Cover and let rise until very light and almost doubled. (Rye rolls take extra rising time.) Brush with a mixture of the remaining egg (beaten) and 1 Tb. water. Bake rolls for 20 to 25 minutes at 350°F. The bottoms overbrown easily, so watch carefully during baking. Makes about 3 dozen rolls.

POTATO ROLLS

Vilma Anderson
McKinley Foothills Bed & Breakfast, Trapper Creek

1 medium potato
1 package yeast
1 cup warm milk (canned milk works better)
2 Tb. sugar
2 tsp. salt
1/2 stick butter
2 beaten eggs (at room temperature)
4¹/₂ to 5¹/₂ cups flour (you can mix some oatmeal flour with
   the white)

Boil potato and save the water. Mix 1 cup potato water with yeast and some flour. Mix well and let stand a few minutes. Mash the potato, and add it to yeast mixture, along with milk, sugar, salt, butter and eggs. Add flour a little bit at a time, until bread dough is elastic and not too sticky. Let it rise until doubled in size. Punch down. Take a chunk and turn it on a floured board and make a flat piece like a pizza. Cut into triangles: first half, then quarters, etc., until it is all cut up into small triangles. Roll them one at a time. Place in a greased baking dish (you can use nonstick spray). Bake for 15 minutes, or until done, at 375°F. Makes 6 to 8. These buns can be frozen, and recipe can be doubled and tripled. Fast yeast can be used, too.

Breads

SOUR CREAM ROLLS

Bob Lee, Manley Roadhouse, Manley Hot Springs

1 package **yeast**
1/2 cup **warm water**
3/4 cup **shortening or butter, softened**
2 **eggs**
1 cup **sour cream at room temperature**
6 cups **flour**
11/2 tsp. **salt**
1/2 cup **sugar**

Preheat oven to 375°F. Dissolve yeast in warm water. Mix together shortening, eggs and sour cream. Add to yeast mixture. Sift together flour, salt and sugar. Add to preceding ingredients. Lightly knead and let rise 1 hour. Shape into rolls. Let rise again, and bake until lightly brown, about 25 minutes. Makes about 4 dozen.

EASY CINNAMON ROLLS

Rita Gittins
Alaskan Frontier Gardens Bed and Breakfast, Anchorage

24 frozen dinner rolls
1 3-oz. package cook-and-serve vanilla pudding
1 cup brown sugar
1/2 cup sugar
4 tsp. cinnamon
1/2 cup chopped pecans (optional)
1/2 cup melted butter (1 cube)

Place 24 frozen dinner rolls in a well-greased bundt pan. Mix together vanilla pudding and brown sugar; pour over rolls. Combine sugar, cinnamon and optional pecans and sprinkle over rolls. Pour melted butter over all. Put bundt pan in oven to rise overnight. In the morning, bake at 350°F for 30 minutes. Let cool for 10 minutes in pan. Turn over on plate, cut and enjoy. Makes 2 dozen.

OVERNIGHT CINNAMON ROLLS

Diane Schoming, Morning Glory Bed & Breakfast, Homer

1 package frozen dinner rolls (about 10 to 15 rolls, or enough
to fill the bottom of pan)
1 3¹/₂-oz. package instant butterscotch pudding
1 cup firmly packed brown sugar
2 Tb. cinnamon
¹/₂ cup melted butter
¹/₂ cup pecans

Layer ingredients in a greased bundt cake pan in the following order: frozen rolls, pudding powder, brown sugar, cinnamon, butter and pecans. Cover the pan with foil topped with a clean towel and allow to sit overnight. Bake in a 350°F oven for 30 minutes. Serves 8 to 10.

FROSTED CINNAMON ROLLS

Carol Rhoades, Gracious House, Mile 82 Denali Highway

Rolls:
4 to 5 cups flour
1 oz. (or 2 packages) powdered yeast
1 cup milk
¹/₃ cup sugar
¹/₃ cup butter
1 tsp. salt
2 eggs
¹/₃ cup brown sugar
¹/₃ cup white sugar
1¹/₂ Tb. cinnamon
raisins (optional)
chopped pecans (optional)

Combine 2 cups flour and yeast, and set aside. In saucepan, heat to milk, ¹/₃ cup sugar, butter and salt to 115°F; don't scald. Add to flour and yeast mixture, and stir. Add eggs and enough of remaining flour to make dough smooth and elastic. Press dough into greased bowl and let double. Cut dough in half and let it rest for 10 minutes. Roll out each half into a rectangle. Spread each with melted butter and top with brown sugar, white sugar and cinnamon, sprinkling evenly and adding raisins and chopped nuts, if desired. Roll up jelly-roll-style and cut each into 8 pieces. Put pieces into pan, cut-side down and with your

Breads

hand smash rolls half-way down. Let rise 45 minutes. Bake at 350°F for 20 to 25 minutes. While still warm, top with cream cheese frosting (see recipe following). Yields 16 rolls.

Frosting:

1 3-oz. package cream cheese, softened
1 Tb. butter
1 tsp. vanilla
2 cups powdered sugar

With an electric mixer at low speed, beat together cream cheese, butter and vanilla. Add sugar gradually, mixing until fluffy.

VICTORIAN HEIGHTS CINNAMON ROLLS

Phil and Tammy Clay
Victorian Heights Bed & Breakfast, Homer

Dough:
1/2 cup **warm water**
1 Tb. yeast
1 tsp. sugar
2 1/2 cups scalded milk
1 cup sugar
1 1/2 tsp. salt
1/2 cup margarine
2 eggs, beaten
7 to 8 cups flour

Filling:
1/2 cup margarine or butter, melted
1 cup brown sugar
2 tsp. cinnamon
nuts and raisins (optional)

Stir water, yeast and sugar together and let set for 10 minutes. In a separate bowl, mix scalded milk, sugar, salt and margarine; let stand until cooled, then add eggs and flour. Add the yeast mixture to this. (You can let this dough stand cov-

ered overnight in the refrigerator, or roll it out after mixing. I have found it easier to mix at night and roll out in the morning. It not only saves preparation time in the morning, but the dough is also easier to work with if it has been refrigerated. This is a very soft, sticky dough, but the soft dough means the rolls will be light.)

Roll out dough on a floured surface; pastry cloth works the best. Pour melted margarine or butter over the rolled out dough. Mix the brown sugar and cinnamon, and sprinkle over buttered dough. Add optional nuts and raisins, if you like.

Roll up dough from the long side and pinch to seal. Cut into 1-inch pieces with dental floss. (Yes, dental floss.) Take a string about 8 inches long and loop it under the end of the dough. Hold the ends of the floss above the dough, and cross over the ends of the floss until it cuts the dough. The floss won't squish and mash the dough like cutting with a knife will. Put pieces side by side in greased cake pan. To make rolls a little lighter, let them rise. Bake at 350°F for 20 to 25 minutes. Makes 2 dozen rolls.

SOURDOUGH CINNAMON BUNS

Grete Perkins,
Trapper John's Bed and Breakfast, Talkeetna

"Finger lickin' good!"

1/4 cup **sugar**
1 cup **flour**
2 tsp. **baking powder**
1/4 tsp. **baking soda**
1/4 tsp. **salt**
1/4 cup **oil**
1 cup **sourdough starter**
3 Tb. **melted butter**
3/4 cup **brown sugar**
1 tsp. **cinnamon**

Mix together sugar, flour, baking powder and baking soda. Add salt, oil and sourdough starter. Knead dough for several minutes. Form dough into a ball, and turn out onto a floured board. Pat into a 9" x 12" rectangle. Brush with melted butter and sprinkle with brown sugar and cinnamon. Roll up and cut into 12 1-inch slices. Place in a greased 9" round pan. Bake at 425°F for 25 minutes, or until golden brown. Makes 12.

CHEESE SCONES

Wenda Lythgoe, The Cabin Bed & Breakfast
Km 219 Haines Highway

4 Tb. butter
1 Tb. honey
1/2 cup plain yogurt OR sour cream
1 egg
1 1/4 cups all-purpose flour
1/2 cup whole-wheat flour
1/2 tsp. baking powder
1/2 tsp. baking soda
1/4 tsp. salt
1/2 cup grated cheese

Preheat oven to 400°F. Place rack in center of oven. Melt butter and honey together, and mix in yogurt and egg. In a medium-size bowl, mix together the flours, baking powder, baking soda and salt. Stir in cheese. Pour egg and yogurt mixture over flour mixture and combine gently with a fork. Don't over mix. Turn out onto a lightly floured surface and fold ingredients together gently a few times. Form into a 6- or 7-inch circle, 1-inch thick. Cut into 6 to 8 pie-shaped wedges and place on ungreased baking pan. Bake 12 to 15 minutes until lightly browned and puffed. Serve immediately with butter and homemade jam.

DOT'S FAMOUS RASPBERRY SCONES

Dot Keith

A Fireweed Hideaway Bed and Breakfast, Fairbanks

"You can use any type of preserves. Instead of making an indentation and adding preserves, you can add chopped-up fruit to the dry ingredients before adding the milk and egg mixture. Then brush with egg white, and add slivered almonds and granulated sugar on the top. Let your imagination run wild. This is a good, basic recipe and the most moist scone I have tried. I freeze them individually in zip-lock bags, and then defrost and reheat in an electric bun warmer to serve at our bed and breakfast."

4 cups **all-purpose flour**

³/₄ cup **sugar**

3 tsp. **baking powder**

1 tsp. **baking soda**

¹/₂ tsp. **salt**

¹/₂ cup **chilled butter,**
   cut in small pieces

1 cup **buttermilk**

1 tsp. **vanilla extract**

¹/₂ tsp. **almond extract**

2 eggs, **lightly beaten**

1 egg white, **beaten until frothy**

2 Tb. **granulated sugar**

¹/₂ cup **raspberry preserves or jam**

P reheat oven to 400° F. Mix together flour, ³/₄ cup sugar, baking powder, baking soda and salt. Cut in butter with a pastry blender until mixture resembles coarse meal. In separate bowl, combine buttermilk, vanilla and almond extracts, and the 2 beaten eggs; add to dry ingredients, stirring until moistened. Mixture will be sticky. Turn out on a lightly floured board and knead 4 to 5 times with floured hands. Pat out 8 rounded palm-size circles. Place on a greased cookie sheet. Press a thumb-size indentation on each scone and brush with beaten egg white. Sprinkle with granulated sugar and fill each indentation with raspberry preserves (or jam). Bake for 18 minutes or until golden brown on top. Serve warm. Serves 8.

MARGAREE SCONES

Norine Shandro, Bed & Breakfast Inn Margaree
Dawson Creek

³/₄ cup **milk**
1 **egg**
3 cups **flour**
3 tsp. **baking powder**
¹/₂ tsp. **salt**
1 cup **currants or raisins**
¹/₂ cup **brown sugar**
³/₄ cup **lard**
white sugar

Beat together milk and egg, and set aside. Mix flour, baking powder, salt, currants or raisins, and brown sugar in a fairly large bowl. Using your fingers, rub the lard into the flour mixture. When well-blended, add milk and egg. Roll to an inch thickness. Cut with biscuit cutter. Sprinkle scones with white sugar. Bake at 350°F for 20 minutes. Makes about 16.

BANNOCK

Fort Nelson Heritage Museum
Mile 300 Alaska Highway

Bannock is a staple food of miners, trappers and other bush travelers in the North. This bannock recipe is a favorite with Fort Nelson residents, who feast on homemade bannock during the community's Heritage Days celebration.

4 cups flour	**2 Tb. baking powder**
2 Tb. sugar	**1 tsp. salt**
3 cups water	**raisins (optional)**

Put all dry ingredients into a bowl and mix. Add water until dough is of dropping consistency. Melt cooking fat in frying pan until hot. Drop tablespoonfuls of mixture into hot fat. Fry until brown all over. Serve with butter and jam. Enjoy! Serves 8 to 10.

SWEET BEAR CLAW

Diane Debigare, Rika's Roadhouse & Landing
Mile 275 Richardson-Alaska Highway

"The best bear claw I've ever tasted," according to one Alaska Highway traveler.

Dough:
1 cup butter
1 Tb. active dry yeast
1/4 cup warm water
3 egg yolks
1/4 cup sugar
1/2 tsp. salt
51/3 oz. evaporated milk
31/2 cups all-purpose flour

White Icing:
91/2 cups powdered sugar
1 Tb. vanilla
2 tsp. almond extract
1/3 cup honey
1 cup milk

Filling:
11/3 cups powdered sugar
1/2 cup margarine, softened
2/3 cup white flour
8 oz. almond paste
3/4 cup almond pieces
1/4 cup raisins
1/4 tsp. cinnamon
2 egg whites
1/2 tsp. vanilla
dash almond extract

For dough, melt butter in a saucepan. Cool. In a mixing bowl, dissolve yeast in warm water. Stir in egg yolks along with sugar, salt, evaporated milk and cooled butter. Add

Breads

the flour to the wet ingredients. Beat with mixer on medium speed until well-blended. Dough will be soft and slightly sticky. Refrigerate dough for 1 to 6 hours. Dough may be frozen for future use.

For filling, cream powdered sugar and margarine. Add flour, almond paste, almond pieces, raisins, cinnamon, egg whites, vanilla and almond extract; mix. Cover and refrigerate until firm (1 to 3 hours).

On a very lightly floured surface, roll out refrigerated dough to a 9-inch by 36-inch rectangle (about 1/4 inch thick). Spread filling evenly over the dough, leaving a 1/2-inch strip uncovered at the top long edge of the dough. Starting with the bottom long edge of the rectangle, roll into a log and pinch edge to make a sealed seam. Roll pinched seam underneath and cut log into 12 equal pieces. Make 3 cuts all the way through each piece, about 2/3 of the width of the dough, to form the "toes." Place paws on baking sheets lined with parchment paper, making sure toes fan out to make a claw. Preheat oven to 350°F (or 300°F for a convection oven) while you let claws proof for 15 minutes. Bake for 15 minutes or until lightly browned.

For icing, mix together all ingredients. When claws have cooled, frost with the icing. Serves 12.

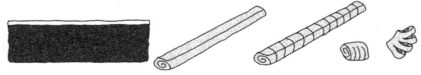

OVERNIGHT COFFEE CAKE

Linda Cline, Cline's Caswell Lake Bed and Breakfast
Mile 88.1 George Parks Highway

2 cups flour
1 tsp. baking powder
1 tsp. baking soda
1 tsp. cinnamon
1/2 tsp. salt
2/3 cup softened margarine
1 cup sugar
1/2 cup brown sugar
2 eggs
1 cup buttermilk

Topping:
1/2 cup brown sugar
1 tsp. cinnamon
1 tsp. nutmeg
1/2 cup chopped nuts (optional)

Combine flour, baking powder, baking soda, cinnamon and salt; set aside. Cream margarine and sugars; add eggs and beat well. Alternate adding dry ingredients and buttermilk to creamed mixture until combined, then spread batter in well-greased 9" x 13" pan. Mix topping ingredients together and spread on top of batter. Cover pan with foil and refrigerate overnight. Bake in preheated 350°F oven for about 45 minutes. Serves 9.

Soups, Salads & Side Dishes

heep Mountain Lodge is a good example of the lodges that sprang up during the 1940s to serve the growing number of motorists coming to Alaska via the Alaska Highway. Located at Mile 113.5 Glenn Highway, Sheep Mountain Lodge opened in 1946, catering to highway traffic and sportsmen. "Here you may have either rooms or private cabins, relax in the cocktail lounge, or enjoy good meals and Alaskan sociability before the big fireplace," read one of their early advertisements. After 50 years, the lodge still caters to highway traffic, offering "rustic charm and old-fashioned Alaskan hospitality."

CREST NORTH COAST FISH SOUP

Chef Wilfred Beaudry, Waterfront Dining Room
Crest Hotel, Prince Rupert

1 litre (approx. 1 qt.) fish stock
$1/2$ tsp. each basil, oregano, thyme, salt
and cracked peppercorns
4 Tb. tomato paste
250 ml (1 cup) white wine
250 grams (8.75 oz.) salmon cubes
250 grams (8.75 oz.) snapper cubes
250 grams (8.75 oz.) halibut cubes
8 prawns
8 clams
$1/2$ Dungeness crab

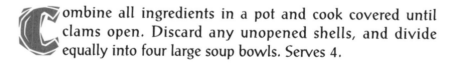

Combine all ingredients in a pot and cook covered until clams open. Discard any unopened shells, and divide equally into four large soup bowls. Serves 4.

HELL'S GATE SALMON CHOWDER

Debbie McKinney, Hell's Gate Airtram, Hope

Fish Stock:
fish frames and trimmings
1 bay leaf
2 carrots, chopped
5 stalks celery, chopped
1 large onion, diced
1 tsp. salt
1/2 tsp. pepper

Chowder:
1 lb. potatoes, cubed
1/2 lb. onions, diced
3/4 head of celery, chopped fine
1 green pepper, diced

1 cup butter
13/4 cups flour
2 qts. milk
2 qts. fish stock
3/4 lb. salmon, minced
1 tsp. pepper
1 Tb. salt
1/2 tsp. season pepper
1/4 tsp. garlic powder
1 tsp. parsley flakes
pinch of thyme
pinch of mace
pinch of bay leaf powder

over fish frames and trimmings, bay leaf, carrots, celery stalks, large onion, 1 tsp. salt and 1/2 tsp. pepper with cold water, bring to a boil, simmer 1 hour and strain. Reserve fish stock. Sauté potatoes, 1/2 lb. of onions, 3/4 head of chopped celery and green pepper in butter. Add flour and stir. Add milk slowly. Add stock. Bring to just under a boil. If too thick, add more stock. Next add salmon and simmer. Lastly add seasoning. Serves 8 to 10.

ALASKAN-STYLE CLAM CHOWDER

Robert Siter, Gwin's Lodge, Mile 52 Sterling Highway

6 cups **milk**
1 large **carrot, shredded**
1¹/₂ stalks **celery, finely chopped**
1 large **potato, finely diced**
2 cups **water**
2 slices **bacon, cooked and finely chopped**
1 medium-sized **onion, finely chopped**
¹/₄ Tb. **ground black pepper**
¹/₈ Tb. **salt**
¹/₄ Tb. **clam base**
12 oz. **chopped clams**
¹/₄ cup **butter**
¹/₄ cup **flour**

our milk into medium-sized saucepan and place over low heat until scalded. Sauté carrot and celery, cooking until almost tender, then add potatoes and water, and cook until tender. Add chopped bacon. In a separate pan, sauté onion and add to vegetable mixture. Add pepper, salt, clam base and chopped clams. In a separate pan, melt butter. Remove from heat and add flour, stirring with whisk until smooth. Pour butter/flour mixture into scalded milk, stirring constantly until smooth. Stir in vegetable mixture. Continue to heat until thoroughly hot. Serves 4.

POTATO CORN CHOWDER

Trapper Creek Inn and General Store, Trapper Creek

"To make a hardier soup, add 2 cups of diced, cooked chicken."

1/4 lb. bacon, diced
1 cup chopped onion
1/2 cup celery
4 cups chicken broth
2 cups peeled potatoes, cut into 1/2-inch cubes
1 10-oz. package frozen corn
1 tsp. salt
1/8 tsp. ground pepper
1/2 pint heavy cream

Fry bacon in large saucepan over medium heat until bacon is brown, about 3 minutes. Add onion and celery, cook 3 more minutes. Stir in broth and bring to a boil over high heat. Add potatoes, corn, salt and pepper. Cook 5 to 10 minutes until potatoes are tender. Stir in cream and reduce heat to low. Cover and simmer 3 minutes. Serve with oyster crackers. Serves 4 to 6.

ITALIAN SAUSAGE SOUP
David Cohen and Diane Schneider
Sheep Mountain Lodge, Mile 113.5 Glenn Highway

1½ lbs. mild Italian sausage, cut into ½-inch-thick slices
2 cloves garlic, minced or pressed
2 large onions, chopped
1 large can (about 28 oz.) Italian-seasoned tomatoes, reserve liquid
3 cans (about 14½ oz. each) beef broth
1½ cups dry red wine OR water
½ tsp. dry basil
3 Tb. chopped parsley
1 medium green bell pepper, seeded and chopped
2 medium zucchini, cut into ½-inch-thick slices
3 cups (about 5 oz.) dry bow-tie pasta
grated parmesan cheese

Cook sausage slices in a deep, 5-quart pan over medium-high heat, stirring often, until lightly browned. Lift out sausage with a slotted spoon and set aside. Discard all but 3 Tb. of fat from the pan. Add garlic and onions to pan; cook over medium heat, stirring often, until onions are soft (about 5 minutes).

Cut up tomatoes; add tomatoes and liquid to pan. Add sausage, broth, wine and basil; stir. Bring to a boil, then reduce heat, cover

and simmer for 20 minutes. Stir in parsley, bell pepper, zucchini and pasta. Cover and simmer, stirring occasionally, until pasta and zucchini are tender to bite (10 to 15 minutes). Skim and discard fat from soup. Serve with parmesan cheese. Serves 6.

KACHEMAK CHOWDER

Jon and Nelda Osgood
Tutka Bay Wilderness Lodge, Homer

1/4 cup **cooking oil**
1 cup **chopped onion**
1 cup **chopped celery**
1/2 tsp. **garlic salt**
1/2 tsp. **dried dill**
2 cups **diced potatoes**
2 cups **sliced carrots**
4 cups **water**
4 cubes **chicken bouillon, or the equivalent**
4 to 6 cups **seafood, precooked or raw, such as chunks of
    halibut, salmon or cod, minced clams, ground octopus,
    shrimp or crab in whatever combination you prefer**
2 cups **canned evaporated milk**
1 can **cream-style corn**
sprigs of fresh dill
fish-shaped crackers

In a 6-quart soup pot, sauté the onion and celery in the oil until soft. Sprinkle with the garlic salt and dill. Add the potatoes and carrots, and sauté for 10 minutes, stirring frequently. Pour in the water, add the bouillon cubes, cover and simmer for 20 minutes, stirring occasionally. When the potatoes and carrots

are tender, add the raw seafood and simmer for 2 to 3 minutes. Then add the cooked seafood. When heated through, add the evaporated milk and corn. Heat, taking care to not let it boil again. Garnish servings with sprigs of fresh dill and fish-shaped crackers. Serves 6 to 8.

MAE'S KITCHEN VEGETABLE BEEF SOUP

Mae's Kitchen, Mile 147 Alaska Highway

At Mae's Kitchen, this soup is served with thick slices of freshly baked, lightly grilled bread.

½ lb. ground beef
1 28-oz. can whole tomatoes
1 48-oz. can tomato juice
6 cups water
1 medium onion, diced
3 cooked potatoes, diced
3 cups frozen mixed vegetables
¼ cup beef soup base
½ tsp. Watkins Soup Spice
(or sage, onion powder, garlic powder, pepper and other spices to taste)

dash of Worcestershire sauce
dash of soy sauce
salt to taste
margarine to taste
brown sugar to taste

Brown meat lightly, drain and set aside. In a large pot, mash tomatoes. Bring tomatoes, juice and water to a boil. Add meat and remaining ingredients. Simmer about 1 hour until done. This soup can be frozen in single-portion servings and used as needed. Serves 8 amply.

GOLD RUSH CABBAGE SOUP

Elvis Presley, The Northern Beaver Post
Mile 649 Alaska Highway

5 strips bacon, chopped
1/4 cup chopped onions
4 Tb. butter OR margarine
pinch cayenne pepper
pinch curry powder
1 tsp. caraway seed
1 tsp. salt
1/2 tsp. pepper
1/2 tsp. parsley
1/4 cup flour
6 cups chopped cabbage
6 cups water
2 Tb. chicken base (or more, to taste)
1 can evaporated milk

Fry bacon and onions in butter. Add spices, flour and cabbage, and cook for 2 minutes. Add water, chicken base and milk, and cook over low heat until soup thickens. Serves 15 to 20 bowls.

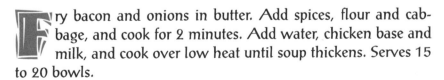

CABIN COLESLAW

Joanne Hawkins, Two Choice Cafe, Nenana

1 small head of cabbage, grated
1 carrot, grated
1 medium-sized onion, diced (optional)
3/4 cup Miracle Whip OR mayonnaise
1 tsp. apple cider vinegar
1 tsp. sugar (more to taste)
1 tsp. yellow mustard
salt, pepper and garlic salt to taste

Mix cabbage, carrot and onion. To Miracle Whip add vinegar, sugar, mustard, salt, pepper and garlic salt. Combine dressing with vegetable mixture and toss well. Serves 6.

Joanne Hawkins traveled to Alaska on her own in the winter of 1970, shooting pool and playing her accordion along the way. She arrived in Nenana with $2 in her pocket. Today, she operates 9 businesses in town, including the Bed and Maybe Breakfast and the Tripod Gift Shop. Her secret? "Hard work, a friendly attitude and good service." She still plays the accordion, and the concertina, entertaining up to 1,000 visitors a day in summer. She also planted and maintains the almost 20,000 flowers that blanket Nenana in summer.

FIDDLEHEAD HOUSE DRESSING

Deborah Marshall, Fiddlehead Restaurant, Juneau

"We've been trying for years to describe this adequately, and there seems to be only one description that fits: indescribably good. Originally made by Joan Daniels at the Bread Factory in Anchorage, this salad dressing has been Alaska's favorite for over 20 years."

1/2 cup **good-quality mayonnaise**
1/2 cup **seeded and coarsely chopped tomatoes**
1/3 cup **coarsely chopped onion (1 small)**
2 Tb. **apple cider vinegar**
2 Tb. **safflower oil**
3 to 4 sprigs **fresh parsley, washed and squeezed dry**
   (about 1/2 Tb. **freshly chopped parsley)**

Place all ingredients in a large blender or food processor. Purée until smooth. Transfer to a 2-cup container, cover and store refrigerated for up to 3 days. Serve with salad or as a vegetable dip. Yields 1 1/2 cups. (Excerpted with permission from "The Fiddlehead Cookbook.")

FIDDLEHEAD VINAIGRETTE

Deborah Marshall, Fiddlehead Restaurant, Juneau

"This is a classic match for green salads, pasta salads or chilled steamed vegetables."

³/₄ cup **good-quality olive oil**
¹/₄ cup **red wine vinegar**
2 tsp. **Dijon mustard**
¹/₂ tsp. **minced garlic (1 small clove)**
¹/₂ tsp. **salt**
¹/₂ tsp. **pepper**
¹/₄ tsp. **dried thyme**

Whisk all ingredients together in a small bowl or pitcher. Store covered for up to 1 week, whisking thoroughly before each use. Yields 1 cup. (Excerpted with permission from "The Fiddlehead Cookbook.")

GRILLED CHICKEN SALAD
The Blues Moose Cafe, Yukon Inn, Whitehorse

3 cups mixed greens
tortilla chips
Honey Lime Dressing
  (recipe follows)
4 4-oz. chicken breasts

12 asparagus spears
Peanut Sauce
  (recipe follows)
1/2 cup feta cheese

Divide mixed greens evenly on 4 plates, surrounding each with about 10 tortilla chips. Drizzle greens with Honey Lime Dressing. Grill chicken and asparagus, and place on top of greens. Drizzle with Peanut Sauce. Top with feta cheese. Serves 4.

Honey Lime Dressing:
1 can frozen lime concentrate
1/4 cup honey mustard sauce
1/4 cup honey
1/4 cup olive oil

2 Tb. garlic
1 Tb. pepper
1/2 cup water

Place all ingredients in blender and blend for 3 minutes.

Peanut Sauce:
1 cup peanut butter
1/2 cup honey (liquid)

1 cup soy sauce
1 cup water

Place all ingredients in blender and blend for 2 minutes.

SEAFOAM SALAD

Jon and Nelda Osgood
Tutka Bay Wilderness Lodge, Homer

1 6-oz. package **lemon or lime gelatin**
2 cups **boiling water**
1¹/₂ cups **pineapple juice (use the juice drained from the canned pineapple)**
2 to 2¹/₂ cups **canned crushed pineapple**
2 cups **creamy cottage cheese**
2 tsp. **horseradish**
1 cup **mayonnaise (may substitute plain nonfat yogurt for some of the mayonnaise)**
¹/₂ cup **chopped walnuts**
1 cup **chopped pimiento-stuffed green olives, drained**
1 cup **diced celery**
parsley

In a medium-sized mixing bowl, dissolve the gelatin in the boiling water. Stir in the pineapple juice. Chill until slightly thickened. With an electric mixer, beat the gelatin until foamy. With a rubber spatula, gently fold in the crushed pineapple, cottage cheese, horseradish, mayonnaise, nuts, olives and celery. Mix well. Pour mixture into a glass serving bowl. Chill until firm (4 to 6 hours). Garnish with several sliced pimiento-stuffed green olives and parsley. Serves 12.

"SECRET INGREDIENT" FRUIT SALAD

Christine & Corbett Upton
Applesauce Inn B&B, Fairbanks

"Despite the utter simplicity of this recipe, guests invariably ask me, 'What's the secret ingredient!'"

4 bananas
1/2 cantalope
1 pint blueberries
1 8-oz. carton lemon yogurt

Dice bananas and cantalope in a large bowl. Add blueberries. Fold in lemon yogurt. Makes 4 large servings or 8 small servings.

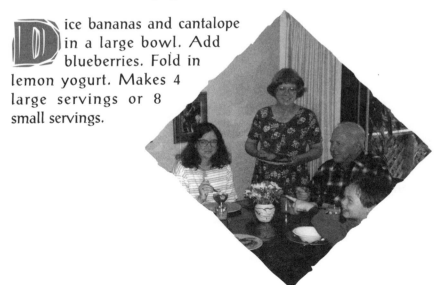

SMOKED SALMON CAESAR SALAD

Deborah Marshall, Fiddlehead Restaurant, Juneau

The world seems to be divided into those who will eat anchovies and those who will not. This variation of the classic Caesar salad brings them together by using smoked salmon instead of anchovies to create a tasty compromise.

16 cups torn, fresh mixed greens (romaine,
leaf lettuce, spinach, rocket, escarole, lamb's lettuce
or other fresh greens)
1/2 lb. Alaskan smoked salmon (not canned), skin
and bones removed
4 tsp. Dijon mustard
1/2 cup Fiddlehead Vinaigrette (see page 120)
2 tsp. minced fresh garlic (2 large cloves)
1 cup garlic-flavored croutons
1/4 cup freshly grated parmesan cheese
16 marinated artichoke hearts
8 tomato slices
8 cucumber slices
16 black olives

Chill 8 salad plates. Place greens in a very large salad bowl. Break smoked salmon into small pieces, and sprinkle it over greens. In a small bowl, whisk together mustard, vinaigrette dressing and garlic. Add dressing mixture, croutons

and cheese to salad bowl. Using your hands or salad tongs, toss salad 30 times or until thoroughly mixed. Divide salad onto the chilled plates and garnish each with artichoke hearts, tomato and cucumber slices, and black olives. Serve salad at once. Serves 8. (Excerpted with permission from "The Fiddlehead Cookbook.")

TROPICAL FRUIT SALAD

Barbara Winkley, Fernbrook Bed & Breakfast, Anchorage

Serve this colorful fruit salad in a glass bowl, garnished with a sprig of mint or decorative flowers, such as pansies. If desired, serve with Lime Sauce or Poppy Seed Dressing (recipes follow) on the side.

3 to 4 pineapple slices
1/2 cantaloupe
1/2 papaya
2 to 3 bananas
1 apple
1 orange, peeled
1 to 2 passion fruit

Dice and mix fruit. (Note: Sprinkle pulp of passion fruit with sugar and freeze to preserve for out-of-season use.) Seasonal fruits, such as strawberries or raspberries, may also be added to this salad.

Lime Sauce:

1 8-oz. package cream cheese, at room temperature
1/3 cup sugar

1/4 cup lime juice
2 Tb. milk

Beat cream cheese with electric mixer at low speed until smooth. Mix in sugar, lime juice and milk until combined. Yields approximately 1 1/2 cups.

Poppy Seed Dressing:
¹/₂ cup **sugar**
1¹/₂ tsp. **minced red or white onion**
¹/₄ tsp. **paprika**
¹/₄ cup **cider vinegar**
¹/₂ cup **vegetable oil**
2 Tb. **sesame seeds**
1 Tb. **poppy seeds**

ix sugar, onion, paprika and cider vinegar together. Whisk in oil until well combined. Add sesame and poppy seeds. Store in refrigerator until ready to use.

PENDLETON POTATOES

Ronald S. Pendleton, Journeymen's B&B, Homer

6 or 7 potatoes, boiled with the jackets on and
   cooled thoroughly (overnight)
1 regular-size can cream of chicken soup
1/2 soup can of milk
1/4 stick of margarine
1 cup sour cream
4 green onions, sliced
1 1/2 cups grated cheddar cheese
Chicken-in-a-Biscuit crackers
melted butter
paprika

Peel and shred potatoes. In a saucepan, heat cream of chicken soup, milk, margarine, sour cream and green onions. Pour 1/3 of this sauce into a 2-qt. casserole dish and add 1/2 of the shredded potatoes. Lightly cover with some of the cheddar cheese. Next, layer another 1/3 of the sauce, the other half of the potatoes and the remaining cheese. Pour the rest of the sauce on top.

Crush some crackers and mix with melted butter. Top potatoes with cracker mixture, and sprinkle lightly with paprika. Bake at 350°F until it bubbles, about 30 minutes.

Main Dishes

ika's Roadhouse, at Mile 275 Richardson Highway, was built by John Hajdukovich, a pioneer prospector, trapper, hunting guide and entrepreneur. The roadhouse opened in 1906, serving the horse-drawn stage line that connected Valdez and Fairbanks. In 1923, Hajdukovich sold it to Rika Wallen, a Swedish immigrant who had managed the roadhouse for him since 1917. Rika ran the roadhouse into the late 1940s, then lived there until her death in 1969 at the age of 94. Alyeska Pipeline Service Co. bought the roadhouse to house pipeline crews during construction of the trans-Alaska pipeline, and later deeded the property to the Delta Historical Society. The society deeded the land to the state of Alaska for a park. Located on 10 acres along the banks of the Tanana River, the roadhouse and historical buildings were renovated and reopened May 28, 1988, as part of Big Delta State Historical Park.

ALASKAN-STYLE SALMON-STUFFED HALIBUT

Robert Siter, Gwin's Lodge, Mile 52 Sterling Highway

1/4 cup **chopped onion**
1/4 cup **chopped celery**
4 Tb. **butter, divided**
1/2 lb. **cooked salmon, flaked**
1/4 cup **dry bread crumbs**
1 tsp. **grated lemon peel**
1/2 tsp. **salt, divided**
pepper
11/2 lb. **halibut fillet, halved**
1/8 tsp. **paprika**
11/2 Tb. **flour**
3/4 cup **half and half**
1/4 cup **white wine**

To prepare stuffing, sauté onion and celery in 2 Tb. butter. Stir in cooked salmon, bread crumbs, lemon peel, 1/4 tsp. salt and dash of pepper. Place half of halibut in a buttered baking dish, sprinkle with paprika and spread salmon stuffing evenly over top. Place the remaining halibut on top of the stuffing. Cover the dish and bake at 425°F for 20 to 25 minutes.

Meanwhile, prepare sauce. Melt 2 Tb. butter in small saucepan and stir in flour, a dash of pepper, a dash of paprika, half and half, and white wine. Stir until thickened.

When halibut is finished cooking, top with white wine sauce and serve. Serves 4.

Main Dishes

GRILLED HALIBUT WITH SUN-DRIED TOMATO SAUCE

Chef Jon Emanuel, Glacier Bay Country Inn, Gustavus

"This is great when served with wild rice and fresh asparagus."

4 7-oz. halibut fillets
1 shallot, chopped
1 oz. white wine vinegar
2 oz. chardonnay
1 oz. cream
$1/2$ lb. cold butter chopped into 1-oz. pats
2 oz. rehydrated sun-dried tomatoes, chopped
$1/2$ oz. fresh basil, chopped
salt and white pepper to taste

Grill fillets over a medium-high heat on a greased grill until done (about 10 minutes per inch of thickness). Meanwhile, in a small saucepan over medium-high heat, boil shallot and vinegar until liquid is almost gone. Add the wine and reduce again until almost dry. Add cream and reduce by half. Turn heat down to low and briskly whisk in butter, one pat at a time, until all is added. Sauce should be smooth and creamy. Strain sauce and return to pot over low heat. Briskly stir in sun-dried tomatoes until sauce has a nice reddish tint. Stir in basil. Season with salt and white pepper. Keep warm (not hot) until ready to spoon over the halibut. Serves 4.

HALIBUT MORNAY

Soldotna Inn and Mykel's Restaurant, Soldotna

Crab Stuffing:
8 oz. crab meat
1 cup bread crumbs
1 Tb. minced shallots
1 tsp. minced roasted garlic
1 Tb. chopped parsley
1/8 tsp. hot sauce
2 egg whites
1/2 cup shredded cheddar cheese

4 8-oz. boneless/skinless halibut fillets
white wine to taste
lemon juice to taste
16 oz. alfredo sauce

Combine all of the crab stuffing ingredients except for half of the cheese in a mixing bowl. Season fillets to taste with your favorite seasonings, white wine and lemon juice. Butterfly halibut fillets and stuff with crab filling. Bake stuffed fillets, covered, at 350°F for approximately 30 minutes. Remove from baking dish. Top with alfredo sauce and remaining cheddar cheese. Glaze under broiler until melted. Serve at once. Serves 4.

HALIBUT SURPRISE

Margie M. Smith
The Bluff House Bed & Breakfast, Ninilchik

"Margie's famous recipe for a great holiday brunch or potluck."

2 cups **halibut (or shrimp, crab or salmon)**
2 cups **grated cheddar cheese**
6 oz. **cream cheese, cubed**
1/2 cup **chopped green onions**
4 cups **milk**
2 cups **Bisquick baking mix**
8 **eggs**
1 1/2 tsp. **salt**

Grease 9" x 13" pan. Layer halibut, cheeses and onion in pan. In blender combine remaining ingredients, or blend 1 minute with a hand beater. Pour into pan. Bake at 400°F for 35 to 40 minutes, or until knife inserted comes out clean. Cool 5 minutes. Serves 6.

HAPPY HALIBUT

Sara Sears, Norlite Campground, Fairbanks

2 lbs. halibut
1/2 lb. scallops
1/2 lb. salad shrimp
1 cup Swiss OR mozzarella
   cheese, shredded
1 package Knorr's Hollandaise
   Sauce Mix
6 to 8 pimiento strips
fresh parsley

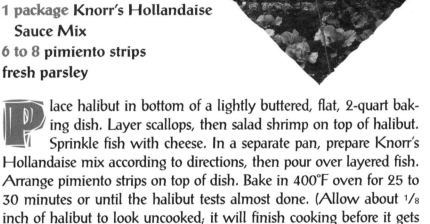

Place halibut in bottom of a lightly buttered, flat, 2-quart baking dish. Layer scallops, then salad shrimp on top of halibut. Sprinkle fish with cheese. In a separate pan, prepare Knorr's Hollandaise mix according to directions, then pour over layered fish. Arrange pimiento strips on top of dish. Bake in 400°F oven for 25 to 30 minutes or until the halibut tests almost done. (Allow about 1/8 inch of halibut to look uncooked; it will finish cooking before it gets to the table.) Garnish with fresh parsley before serving. Serves 6 to 8. (Excerpted with permission from "Sara's Alaskan Seafood Secrets.")

Anyone who has ever stayed at Norlite Campground in Fairbanks would know Sara, if only by the "Love Sara" signs that appear throughout the campground. It has been said in jest that Sara is her middle name, her full-name being "Love Sara 5 mph." She is author of "Have You Hugged A Tourist Lately!", about her experiences running a campground for 30 years.

HOMESTEAD HALIBUT

Jean Somers, Homestead House B&B
Mile 135 Sterling Highway

1/2 cup butter
1 garlic clove, chopped
1 large onion, chopped
1 cup soy sauce
1/4 cup sugar
2 lbs. halibut

In a frying pan, cook garlic and onion in butter. Add soy sauce and sugar, and cook until sugar is dissolved. Place halibut in cake pan and pour sauce over fish. Cook fish on barbecue or bake in 350°F oven for 20 minutes or until halibut flakes when tested with a fork. Serves 6.

UNFORGETTABLE HALIBUT
(OR CRAB OR SHRIMP OR TUNA)
Sara Sears, Norlite Campground, Fairbanks

"This is one that impressed my mother's bridge group. I serve it with a fruit salad and a soft dinner roll. Talk about easy living!"

4 Tb. butter	1 can cream of mushroom soup
1/2 cup chopped onion	1 cup light cream
1 1/2 cups sliced mushrooms	3 cups cooked rice
1 cup chopped celery	1/2 cup slivered almonds
1 lb. cooked halibut OR	1 tsp. curry powder
3 cans crab, shrimp or tuna	2 tsp. fresh ground pepper
1 cup mayonnaise	2 cups buttered bread crumbs

Melt butter in heavy saucepan and sauté onion, mushrooms and celery. In a large bowl, combine halibut (or crab, shrimp or tuna) with mayonnaise, mushroom soup, cream, rice, almonds, curry powder and pepper. Stir in sautéed vegetables and pour mixture into a large buttered casserole, topping with buttered bread crumbs. Bake uncovered at 350°F for 30 to 40 minutes. Serves 12. (Excerpted with permission from "Sara's Alaskan Seafood Secrets.")

BBQ SALMON

Sandy Grunow, Sergeant Preston's Lodge, Skagway

³/₄ cup brown sugar
¹/₄ cup salt
¹/₄ cup cooking oil
¹/₄ cup vinegar
whole salmon

Mix together sugar, salt, cooking oil and vinegar. Open fish down center, preferably not separating skin along back. Spread sauce on fish and allow at least ¹/₂ hour to marinate. Put salmon on tin foil and place in barbecue. Once well heated up, turn barbecue down a little. Cook approximately 1 hour. Serves 6 to 10.

BROCCOLI SALMON CASSEROLE

Laurie Coates
Almost Home Bed & Breakfast/Cabins, Homer

"Delicious casserole — especially for those of us who don't particularly care for salmon."

1/2 cup **chopped onion**
1 Tb. **butter**
1 8-oz. can **cream of celery soup**
1 4-oz. can **mushrooms, drained**
3/4 cup **grated parmesan cheese**
1/2 tsp. **dill**
1/2 tsp. **salt**
1/4 tsp. **pepper**
2 Tb. **lemon juice**
10 oz. **broccoli spears, cooked**
3/4 cup **cooked, flaked salmon**

Sauté onion in butter until tender. Add soup and mix ingredients together. Add mushrooms, cheese, dill, salt, pepper and lemon juice. Mix well. Toss in broccoli and salmon. Pour in shallow, buttered baking dish. Bake at 350°F for 20 minutes. Serves 4.

COPPER RIVER SALMON CHILI

Margy Johnson, Reluctant Fisherman Inn, Cordova

If Copper River king salmon is unavailable, use whatever salmon you can find.

1¹/₂ cups **dried kidney beans**
¹/₄ cup **olive oil**
¹/₂ tsp. **cayenne pepper**
1 tsp. **ground cumin**
1 tsp. **dried oregano**
2 Tb. **chopped garlic**
¹/₂ cup **diced green pepper**
1 cup **diced celery**

1 cup **diced white onion**
4 cups **canned, diced tomatoes packed in purée**
2 Tb. **chili powder, or to taste**
2 lbs. **Copper River king salmon, skinned and boned**
2 cups **grated cheddar cheese**

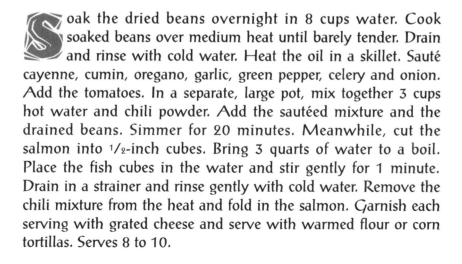

oak the dried beans overnight in 8 cups water. Cook soaked beans over medium heat until barely tender. Drain and rinse with cold water. Heat the oil in a skillet. Sauté cayenne, cumin, oregano, garlic, green pepper, celery and onion. Add the tomatoes. In a separate, large pot, mix together 3 cups hot water and chili powder. Add the sautéed mixture and the drained beans. Simmer for 20 minutes. Meanwhile, cut the salmon into ¹/₂-inch cubes. Bring 3 quarts of water to a boil. Place the fish cubes in the water and stir gently for 1 minute. Drain in a strainer and rinse gently with cold water. Remove the chili mixture from the heat and fold in the salmon. Garnish each serving with grated cheese and serve with warmed flour or corn tortillas. Serves 8 to 10.

SALMON ORIENTAL

Lillian Banaszak
The Chilkat Restaurant and Bakery, Haines

1¹/₂ cups soy sauce
1 cup olive oil
¹/₄ cup red wine
4 garlic cloves, crushed
1 tsp. black pepper
3 cups thinly sliced onion
2 sockeye salmon fillets, deboned and cut into 1-inch strips
3 cups red and green bell peppers, julienned

Mix soy sauce, oil, wine, garlic, pepper and onion. Pour marinade over salmon and let sit for at least 4 hours. Grill in olive oil over medium heat until salmon is almost cooked. Then add the peppers and finish cooking. Serve over rice. Serves 6.

SPICY SALMON PATTIES

Carol Harmon, Harmony Bed & Breakfast, Seward

"These patties freeze well, so you can enjoy them all winter long."

³/₄ lb. poached, flaked salmon
¹/₂ cup bread crumbs
1 Tb. barbecue sauce
1 Tb. mayonnaise
1 tsp. cajun spice
1 egg
salt, pepper and garlic powder to taste

 ix all ingredients with hands until well blended. Shape into 4 patties. Fry in margarine until golden brown on both sides. Serve warm with favorite seafood sauce. Serves 4.

BAKED GINGER LIME SALMON

Lisa Wax, Tsaina Lodge, Mile 34.7 Richardson Highway

"The old-timers who still frequent the lodge prefer a simple salmon preparation that doesn't overpower the natural, delicate flavor of the Copper River salmon."

4 limes
¹/₄ cup brown sugar
¹/₄ cup soy sauce
¹/₄ cup sesame oil
1 Tb. grated fresh ginger
4 8-oz. salmon filets

Zest and juice limes. Add brown sugar, soy sauce, sesame oil and ginger. Mix well. Marinate salmon for 1 hour or overnight. Transfer salmon with marinade to an oven-safe baking pan. Bake at 375°F for 15 to 20 minutes. Serves 4.

SCAMPI LAKE LOUISE STYLE

Glen Miles, Lake Louise Lodge, Lake Louise

"This is our house specialty."

2 Tb. butter
2 Tb. margarine
1 dash cayenne pepper
juice from 1/4 fresh lemon
1 tsp. Worcestershire sauce
1 clove crushed garlic
1 dash salt
1/4 carrot
2 slices onion
1/4 green pepper,
  seeded and sliced
1/4 red pepper,
  seeded and sliced

2 broccoli crowns,
  broken into florets
1/2 stalk celery, chopped
2 cauliflower clusters,
  broken into florets
2 Tb. white wine
12 Alaskan spotted shrimp
  (or scallops)
1 Tb. butter
2 slices tomato
2 sprigs parsley
lemon wedges
1 dash paprika

Melt 2 Tb. butter and margarine, and add cayenne, lemon juice, Worcestershire sauce, garlic and salt. Sauté vegetables, except tomatoes, for 5 minutes. Add white wine. Add shrimp, and simmer slowly for 3 to 5 minutes until shrimp are barely done. Add 1 Tb. butter. Put into bowl, and garnish with tomato, parsley and lemon wedges. Sprinkle very lightly with paprika. Serve with baked potato. Serves 2.

CRAB CAKES

Karen Eldridge
Paxson Lodge, Mile 185.5 Richardson Highway

8 oz. crab meat, broken into small pieces
20 soda crackers, crushed
2 Tb. mayonnaise
1 tsp. Tabasco sauce
1 Tb. lemon juice
1/4 small onion, chopped finely
2 eggs, well beaten
1/8 tsp. sage
salt and pepper to taste

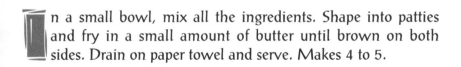

In a small bowl, mix all the ingredients. Shape into patties and fry in a small amount of butter until brown on both sides. Drain on paper towel and serve. Makes 4 to 5.

PEPPER CRAB CAKES

Chef La Mont Caldwell, Alyeska Resort, Girdwood

Chef La Mont Caldwell is responsible for creating menus and specials for Alyeska Resort's mountain-top Seven Glaciers Restaurant. These crab cakes are served on a bed of corn purée with a cilantro-lime sauce and garnish.

16 oz. fresh or frozen Dungeness crab meat

1 each red, yellow and green bell pepper, rinsed and diced (reserve half for garnish)

¹/₄ bunch fresh cilantro (save 4 sprigs for garnish)

1 lemon, zested

¹/₄ cup mayonnaise

Panko bread crumbs

salt

white pepper

olive oil

Corn Purée (recipe follows)

Cilantro-Lime Sauce (recipe follows)

Squeeze crab meat well to remove all excess liquid. Place in bowl and toss to break up some of the larger pieces. Add half of the diced and rinsed bell peppers. Coarsely chop cilantro and add to bowl. Add lemon zest and mayonnaise. Combine all ingredients. Check consistency: Mixture should have the same texture as tuna salad. If too dry, add more mayonnaise. Bind together with Panko bread crumbs. Form into 8 equal-size balls and roll outside in bread crumbs; form into cakes.

You can make your mixture a day in advance, refrigerate and bread just before cooking.

In sauté pan, heat 1 oz. olive oil, cook crab cakes until golden brown on both sides. Remove from pan. Place on paper towels to absorb excess oil. Place 1¹/₂ oz. warm Corn Purée (recipe follows) in center of each of 4 plates. Arrange crab cakes so that one is flat in center of purée and the other leans against it at a 45° angle. Drizzle with Cilantro Lime Sauce (recipe follows) in a zigzagging method. Garnish with fresh small-diced green, yellow and red bell pepper, and fresh sprig of cilantro. Serves 4.

Corn Purée:

1 8-oz. can corn purée	cayenne, chili powder,
2 oz. heavy cream	paprika, salt, white
2 oz. water	pepper to taste

Place corn, cream and water in a saucepan, bring to a simmer. Add spices to taste. Simmer to oatmeal consistency. Hold until ready to serve.

Cilantro-Lime Sauce:

6 limes, zested and juiced	¹/₂ cup olive oil
¹/₄ cup Chardonnay vinegar	1 bunch chopped cilantro
1 egg	

Combine lime juice, vinegar and egg in blender. Blend at medium speed while drizzling in olive oil to emulsify. Place in mixing bowl and add fresh chopped cilantro, salt and pepper to taste. Add fresh lime zest.

Main Dishes

ARCTIC DIP

Sherry Berryman, H & H Lakeview Restaurant
Mile 99.5 George Parks Highway

"We are located on the Parks Highway, and we have some loyal customers in Fairbanks 260 miles away who insist that this sandwich is worth the drive!"

**5 to 6 oz. boneless rump roast, cooked rare and
sliced wafer-thin**
**1 6-inch sourdough roll, sliced in half and lightly brushed
with melted butter**
3 whole onion slices, thinly sliced and sautéed in butter
1 to 2 oz. Swiss cheese, sliced
3/4 cup juice from roast
3/4 cup water

Put the sliced beef in a hot pan and toss gently until thoroughly warm. Place the beef as a layer on one side of the sourdough roll, add sautéed onions and top with Swiss cheese. Warm roast juice and water in a saucepan. Place the sandwich, open-faced, under a broiler until the cheese is bubbly. Put the top on the sandwich and cut diagonally. Serve with au jus. We prefer to add some crispy french fries and some of our creamy coleslaw as side dishes to this meal. Serves 1.

DAWSON PEAKS BEEF BURRITOS

Carolyn Allen
Dawson Peaks Resort, Mile 797 Alaska Highway

"Serve with a fresh garden salad and refried beans."

1 lb. ground beef	1/2 tsp. dried jalapeño pepper
6 oz. crushed tomatoes	1 cup salsa
1/4 tsp. salt	4 to 6 8-inch flour tortillas
1 tsp. chili powder	grated Monterey Jack cheese
1 tsp. crushed red chili pepper	jalapeño peppers
1/4 tsp. cayenne pepper	chopped fresh tomatoes
1 Tb. flour	sour cream

Brown meat and drain. Add crushed tomatoes and stir together with beef. Blend salt, chili powder, red chili pepper, cayenne and flour together in 1/4 cup of cold water to make a paste. Add this paste to the beef mixture along with the diced jalapeño peppers. Cook slowly and stir frequently for 20 to 30 minutes. Fill warmed tortillas with approximately 1/2 cup of the meat mixture and 1 Tb. of salsa. Roll and wrap tortillas, and garnish with Monterey Jack cheese, jalapeño peppers, tomatoes and sour cream. Serves 4.

CALIFORNIA MEAT CLAW

Diane Debigare, Rika's Roadhouse & Landing
Mile 275 Richardson-Alaska Highway

Filling:
1¹/₂ oz. dried tomato halves, chopped
   (approximately 15 halves)
³/₄ cup provolone cheese, cut into ¹/₄-inch cubes
³/₄ cup mozzarella cheese, cut into ¹/₄-inch cubes
1¹/₂ cups grated parmesan
3 oz. pepperoni, cut into ¹/₄-inch strips
¹/₂ cup plus 1 Tb. sour cream   ¹/₂ tsp. salt
2 Tb. olive oil   1¹/₂ Tb. basil
1¹/₂ cups chopped onions   1¹/₂ Tb. oregano
¹/₄ oz. garlic, minced   ¹/₄ tsp. thyme

Dough:
3¹/₂ to 4 cups white flour   ¹/₂ tsp. salt
1 package active dry yeast   2 egg yolks
1 cup water   1 slightly beaten egg yolk
¹/₄ cup margarine   3 Tb. cold water

Soak tomatoes in boiling water for 5 minutes, then drain. Add provolone, mozzarella, parmesan, pepperoni and sour cream to tomatoes, and mix. In skillet over medium heat, heat olive oil and sauté onion, garlic and salt. Crush the basil,

oregano and thyme as you sprinkle them into the skillet. Add sautéed seasonings to the tomato mixture and mix well. Chill 1 to 3 hours before spreading.

For dough, combine 1¹/₂ cups flour and the yeast in a mixing bowl, and set aside. In a saucepan, heat and stir the water, margarine and salt until just warm (110°F to 120°F) and the margarine almost melts. Add this to the flour mixture; then add 2 egg yolks. Beat on low to medium speed for 30 seconds, scraping sides of bowl. Add remaining flour and beat on high speed for 3 minutes to have a moderately stiff dough that is smooth and elastic. Shape into a ball, cover and let rise until double. Punch dough down.

On a very lightly floured surface, roll dough to a 9-inch by 36-inch rectangle (about ¹/₄ inch thick). Spread filling evenly over the dough, leaving a ¹/₂-inch strip uncovered at the top long edge of the dough. Starting with the bottom long edge of the rectangle, roll into a log and pinch edge to make a sealed seam (see illustration on page 105). Roll pinched seam underneath and cut log into 12 equal pieces. Make 3 cuts all the way through each piece, about ²/₃ of the width of the dough, to form the "toes." Place paws on baking sheets lined with parchment paper, making sure toes fan out to make a claw. Mix together 1 egg yolk and 3 Tb. cold water, and brush over each claw. Preheat oven to 350°F (or to 300°F for a convection oven) while you let claws proof for 15 minutes. Bake for 15 minutes or until lightly browned. Serves 12.

FAMOUS MILE 649ER BBQ RIBS

Elvis Presley, The Northern Beaver Post
Mile 649 Alaska Highway

5 to 10 lbs. ribs (plan on about 1 lb. of ribs per serving)
1/2 cup brown sugar
juice and pulp of 6 oranges OR 1/4 cup frozen orange juice
   concentrate (do not add water)
1 cup ketchup

1/4 tsp. paprika	1/2 cup water
1/4 tsp. pepper	1 Tb. corn starch
1 tsp. curry powder	2 Tb. vinegar
1/4 cup chopped onions	1 Tb. Worcestershire sauce
1 Tb. margarine	2 Tb. soy sauce

Boil ribs until meat shrinks from bone. While ribs are boiling, mix together brown sugar, orange juice and pulp (or frozen concentrate), ketchup, paprika, pepper and curry powder for barbecue sauce. Set aside. When ribs are ready, add onions, margarine, water, corn starch, vinegar, Worcestershire sauce and soy sauce, and simmer for 1 to 1 1/2 hours. Remove ribs from water. Coat completely with barbecue sauce and bake at 350°F until sauce is thick and gooey, about 2 hours.

HERITAGE HOUSE STEW

Hudson's Bay 1881 Heritage House Restaurant, Quesnel

"This is not a fast food. Allow yourself 3 hours of cooking time."

6 to 7 lbs. chuck steak	2 cups turnips
2 Tb. oil	2 cups diced celery
6 cups cubed carrots	2 cups chopped onion
1 Tb. salt	2 cups tomato sauce
2 tsp. pepper	1/2 cup margarine
1 Tb. sugar	1/2 cup flour

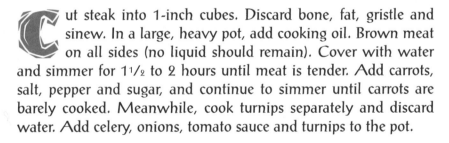

Cut steak into 1-inch cubes. Discard bone, fat, gristle and sinew. In a large, heavy pot, add cooking oil. Brown meat on all sides (no liquid should remain). Cover with water and simmer for 1 1/2 to 2 hours until meat is tender. Add carrots, salt, pepper and sugar, and continue to simmer until carrots are barely cooked. Meanwhile, cook turnips separately and discard water. Add celery, onions, tomato sauce and turnips to the pot.

To prepare the gravy, combine margarine and flour in heavy skillet. Cook over low heat, stirring constantly until mixture is a rich brown color. Add liquid from the stew to form a thick gravy. Return gravy to the stew pot. Mix all ingredients gently. Add water, salt and pepper if required. Let simmer for 5 to 10 minutes before serving. Serve with mashed or boiled potatoes and baking powder biscuits. Serves 15 to 20.

FILET OF BEEF, THREE TOMATO CRUDITÉ

Chef La Mont Caldwell, Alyeska Resort, Girdwood

This beef filet is served on a bed of chard and onion and topped with tomato crudité. You may wish to serve with roasted mashed potatoes and a veal demi sauce drizzled in a zigzag design around the plate.

4 8-oz.beef filets	**White Chard/Sweet Onion (recipe follows)**
salt	**Tomato Crudité (recipe follows)**
black pepper	

Season beef filets with salt and black pepper. Grill or barbecue. Heat White Chard/Sweet Onion mixture in a sauté pan with 1 oz. olive oil. Place equal portions in center of 4 plates; rest beef filet on top. Cover with 2 oz. Tomato Crudité on each filet. Serves 4.

White Chard/Sweet Onion:
2 yellow onions
2 bunches white chard (fresh spinach may be substituted)
salt, white pepper

Peel and julienne onion, and sauté over low heat in pan with 1 oz. olive oil until onion is translucent and tender. Clean chard, and remove stem and stalk with a paring knife. Add to onion and cook until wilted and tender. Season with salt and white pepper. Remove from pan and cool until ready to serve.

Main Dishes

Three Tomato Crudité:

1 large, ripe, red tomato
1 large, ripe, yellow tomato
4 to 5 tomatillos (small green) tomatoes
1 red onion, diced small
1 Tb. minced garlic
2 Tb. minced capers (plus 1 Tb. caper juice)
2 lemons, zested and juiced
2 Tb. grated parmesan cheese
chopped fresh basil, thyme
and oregano to taste
1/4 cup olive oil
salt, white pepper

Dice all tomatoes and place in bowl. Add onion, garlic, capers and caper juice. Mix together with lemon zest and juice, cheese and herbs. Add olive oil, and season with salt and white pepper. Do not over mix crudité. Over mixing will destroy the tomatoes. Adjust consistency by adding or decreasing olive oil. It should be a thick, chunky consistency.

The centerpiece of Alyeska Resort is the chateau-style Westin Alyeska Prince Hotel (pictured above), which has 2 restaurants: the Katsura Teppanyaki Japanese steak house and the Pond Cafe. The executive chef for Alyeska Resort is Al Levinsohn.

PAPRIKA BEEF ROLLS

Cheryl Dutka, Sportsman Inn
Pink Mountain, Alaska Highway

3 (about 1 lb. each) round steaks
salt
pepper
paprika
1/2 lb. mushrooms, sliced
onions, sliced thinly
pimiento, chopped
stuffed olives, sliced

dried bread crumbs
1/2 cup melted butter
1 Tb. boiling water
1 egg
flour
6 whole mushrooms
2 small onions
1 cup red wine

Pound steaks until thin; rub in salt, pepper and paprika to taste. Overlap steaks, making 1 large steak. Spread with layer of mushrooms, onions, pimiento, olives and a light sprinkling of bread crumbs. With whisk, combine butter, boiling water and egg. Immediately dribble mixture over bread crumbs. Roll meat up and tie firmly with string. Flour the outside and brown in butter. Place steak in roaster pan with whole mushrooms and small onions. Sprinkle lightly with salt, pepper and paprika. Add red wine. Bake in 350°F oven for about 2 hours. Serves 6.

SWISS STEAK

Lisa Ashby, Copper Center Lodge, Copper Center

"This dish is absolutely delicious, out-of-this-world, quick and easy to make, budget-effective, appealing to all ages, and it melts in your mouth; steak knives not required."

6 6-oz. cube steaks
1 cup flour
1 medium onion, seeded and sliced
2 green peppers, sliced
1/4 lb. carrots, sliced
1 No. 303 can tomato sauce
2 cloves garlic, minced
2 Tb. parsley flakes
2 Tb. Worcestershire sauce
2 Tb. lemon juice

redge cube steaks in flour and brown in hot, greased skillet. Place on racks in roasting pan. Layer onions, green peppers and carrots on browned steaks. Combine tomato sauce, garlic, parsley flakes, Worcestershire sauce and lemon juice in a saucepan. Bring to a boil and simmer uncovered for 15 minutes. Pour sauce over meat and vegetables. Cover pan with aluminum foil and bake at 350°F for 1 1/2 hours. Serves 6.

Main Dishes

TRULY TENDER PORK CHOPS

Jan Thacker, Coldfoot Services and Arctic Acres Inn, Coldfoot

6 center-cut pork chops
1 egg, beaten
Italian-seasoned bread crumbs
1 large can pear halves and juice

Trim all fat from chops. Tenderize with meat hammer until thin. Dip in beaten egg, and coat with bread crumbs. Brown in butter or margarine until golden brown. Place in a 9" x 13" pan, and pour pear juice around chops. Place pear halves around chops. Cover with foil, and bake at 350°F for 30 to 40 minutes. Serves 6.

BIRCH BARBECUED CHICKEN

Susan Humphrey, Mile 18 Haines Highway

Susan Humphrey's recipe uses her own product, Birch Boy Alaskan Birch Syrup. "The birch boy, Evan Humphrey (pictured below), is also known as the 'yellow-haired sap-sicle sucker,'"writes Susan.

whole fryer chicken, cleaned and cut in pieces OR
  4 boneless, skinless chicken breasts
3/4 cup birch syrup
3/4 cup olive oil
1 clove garlic, finely minced
1 tsp. cumin
1 tsp. onion salt
freshly ground black pepper

After cleaning and drying chicken, mix all other ingredients in a glass or plastic container. Add chicken and mix thoroughly with your hands. (This is messy, but it tenderizes the meat and ensures good contact with the marinade.) Cover container and place in refrigerator. Allow meat to marinate at least 24 hours. Remove chicken from marinade and barbecue over hot coals, with a few twigs of green birch, until golden on the outside and cooked through to center. Serves 4.

MOOSE CREEK CHICKEN
Chef George Stone (a.k.a. Chicken George),
Kantishna Roadhouse, Denali National Park

"This recipe was originally known as '40 Below Chicken.'"

Marinade:
1 qt. liquid smoke
1/2 gallon water
1/4 cup crushed garlic
1/2 cup brown sugar
1/4 cup black pepper, cracked
48 pieces of chicken
2 cups flour

Barbecue sauce:
1/4 cup salad oil
1/2 cup bourbon
1/2 cup sherry
3 dashes soy sauce
3 dashes Worcestershire sauce
4 cloves crushed garlic
1 Tb. black pepper
1 cup brown sugar
1/2 cup molasses
1/2 gallon catsup

6 oz. tomato paste
2 tsp. dry mustard

For marinade, mix together the liquid smoke, water, 1/4 cup garlic, 1/2 cup brown sugar and 1/4 cup pepper. Marinate chicken in marinade sauce no longer than 45 minutes. Remove chicken from marinade and cook in oven for 15 minutes at 325°F. Pull chicken out of oven and dredge in flour. Place back in oven and cook for 15 minutes.

For barbecue sauce, mix together oil, bourbon, sherry, soy sauce, Worcestershire sauce, 4 cloves crushed garlic, 1 Tb. pepper, 1 cup brown sugar, molasses, catsup, tomato paste and mustard.

Pull chicken back out of oven and dip in barbecue sauce, place back in oven for 20 minutes, or until it reaches a temperature of 185°F. Serves 48.

PEACE COUNTRY CHICKEN

Charles Kux-Kardos, Alaska Cafe & Dining Room
Dawson Creek

4 boneless chicken breasts
8-oz. black forest ham
4 spinach leaves
4 oz. mushrooms, sliced
flour
vegetable oil
bread crumbs

Eggwash:
1 egg
1 tsp. water
combine with wire whisk

Place chicken between two pieces of plastic wrap and pound to even thickness with a wooden mallet. Place equal portions of ham, spinach and mushrooms in middle of each chicken breast and roll, making certain that the ends are tucked inside. Bread rolled chicken by dipping in eggwash, then flour, back into the eggwash and then into the bread crumbs. (Note that chicken is easier to bread when still slightly frozen.) Brown chicken in frying pan in 1 inch of vegetable oil, or use a clean deep-fryer. Bake at 325°F for 20 minutes. Serve with a Florentine sauce. Serves 4.

Main Dishes

The distinctive Alaska Hotel, Cafe & Pub is located "55 paces" from Milepost 0 of the Alaska Highway in Dawson Creek, British Columbia. It is owned and operated by Charles and Heidy Kux-Kardos, who purchased the cafe in 1972 and the hotel in 1989. The hotel building dates from the 1930s and the cafe from the 1950s. Charles and Heidy refurbished both establishments and have concentrated on offering fine dining in the Canadian North.

A lover of old cars, Charles Kux-Kardos still owns the first car he ever bought, a 1929 Plymouth Coupe purchased in 1960 when he was 15 years old. In honor of the Alaska Highway's 50th anniversary in 1992, Kux-Kardos led a group of Rolls-Royce and Bentley motorcars up the Alaska Highway. He completed the "Smooth Cruise," as the Alaska Highway trip was dubbed, driving his own Rolls-Royce, a 1956 Silver Cloud I named Princess Daisy.

TOMATO-BASIL CHICKEN

Camp Denali and North Face Lodge, Denali National Park

"Serve with linguini tossed in garlic-parmesan butter and chopped parsley."

1¹/₃ cup **olive oil**
¹/₂ cup **balsamic vinegar**
1 cup **red wine**
1 tsp. **oregano**
2 Tb. **minced garlic**
1 Tb. plus ¹/₂ tsp. **each salt and pepper, divided**
10 **chicken breasts, skinned and cut in half**
1 cup **onions and/or leeks, chopped**
2 cups **mushrooms, sliced thick**
5 lbs. **canned whole tomatoes,**
   broken or chopped and drained
¹/₂ cup **fresh basil, chopped**
¹/₂ cup **fresh parsley, chopped**

Combine 1 cup olive oil, vinegar, ¹/₂ cup of the red wine, oregano, 1 Tb. of the garlic, ¹/₂ tsp. salt and ¹/₂ tsp. pepper. Allow flavors to infuse for several hours. Prepare chicken breasts by laying them closely in baking pans. Pour marinade over them. Cover with foil and store in cool place for at least 3 hours.

Sauté onions and the other 1 Tb. of garlic in the other ¹/₃ cup

olive oil. Add mushrooms and sauté until mushrooms sweat. Add tomatoes, basil, parsley, and the remaining 1 Tb. salt, 1 Tb. pepper and 1/2 cup red wine. Simmer together just enough to mingle flavors, 10 to 15 minutes. Allow to sit in a cool place at least several hours or overnight.

Preheat oven to 375°F. Before cooking, turn chicken pieces in marinade, then re-cover. Cook chicken, covered, 30 minutes in small pans or 40 minutes in large pans. Heat tomato sauce slowly in 2 separate pots (to keep hot while serving). Serve chicken topped with heaping spoonful of tomato sauce. Serves 10. (This recipe can be multiplied by 4 to serve 40, and by 6 to serve 60.)

SOUPER EASY CHICKEN ENCHILADAS

Jan Lawson, Reindeer Mountain Lodge, Cantwell

2 10½-oz. cans cream of chicken soup
1 pint sour cream
1 4-oz. can diced green chilies
1 4-oz. can sliced mushrooms
1 2½-oz. can sliced olives
2 10-oz. cans chicken
2 Tb. vegetable oil
12 to 14 corn tortillas
1 lb. each Monterey Jack and cheddar cheese,
   grated and combined

Preheat oven to 350°F. Mix cream of chicken soup, sour cream, green chilies, mushrooms, olives and chicken in bowl and set aside. Heat oil in fry pan. Dip each tortilla into hot oil until softened, drain on paper towel. Spread a thin layer of creamed mixture in bottom of a 9" x 12" pan. Spread creamed mixture down the middle of each tortilla, top with grated cheese, roll and place seam-side-down in pan. Reserve some of the creamed mixture and grated cheese and spread over the top of all tortillas when pan is filled. Bake 25 to 30 minutes. Serve with sliced jalapeños. Serves 6 to 8.

Main Dishes

NORTH POLE COFFEE'S FAMOUS CHILI

LeOrla Wright & Joy Ford,
North Pole Coffee House, North Pole

4 cans (30 oz. each) vegetarian chili beans
2 cups crushed tomatoes
2 shots espresso
cumin
garlic
seasoning salt
Tabasco
shredded cheese
onions
jalapeño peppers

Pour chili beans, tomatoes and espresso into a slow cooker. Season with cumin, garlic, salt and Tabasco to taste. Let simmer for 3 to 4 hours, stirring occasionally. Serve with shredded cheese, onions and jalapeño peppers. Serves 15 to 20.

BEEF OR VEGETABLE LASAGNA

Carol Rhoades, Gracious House Lodge
Mile 82 Denali Highway

2 lbs. hamburger*
1 cup chopped onion
1 cup chopped celery
1 cup chopped green pepper
1 6-oz. can tomato paste
2 15-oz. cans Italian tomatoes
3 15-oz. cans tomato sauce
2 cups canned or fresh mushrooms
1/2 cup red wine
parsley, oregano, minced garlic, black pepper and other
    seasonings you like, to taste
3/4 box (12-oz. size) lasagna noodles, place in pan uncooked
15 oz. low-fat cottage cheese OR ricotta (or both)
1 cup fresh parmesan cheese
2 cups reduced-fat mozzarella cheese
1/2 cup cheddar cheese

   * Hamburger can be replaced with 1 cup each steamed cauliflower,
zucchini, yellow squash, spinach and carrots.

rown hamburger, onions, celery and green pepper. Add tomato paste, tomatoes, tomato sauce, mushrooms, red wine and spices, and cook slowly for 2 hours. When sauce is finished, cover bottom of a 6" x 14" dish with a thin layer of sauce. Place a layer of noodles over sauce, then cottage cheese, parmesan, mozzarella and cheddar cheeses, and sauce. Repeat so there are 2 to 3 layers. Refrigerate overnight. Bake at 400°F for 1 hour. Let cool 30 minutes. Serves 16.

Desserts

opper Center Lodge, on the Richardson Highway in Copper Center, had its beginnings as the Holman Hotel, and was known as the Blix Roadhouse during the gold rush days of 1897-98. It was the first lodging place in the Copper River Valley, and was replaced by the Copper Center Lodge in 1932, after the original structure burned down. The historic lodge offers 21 rooms with private or shared baths, and a restaurant serving century-old sourdough starter.

Desserts

ALASKA RHUBARB PIE

Susan and Ken Risse
The Blue Goose Bed & Breakfast, Fairbanks

"This is a dessert, but we always serve it at breakfast. It is our specialty."

Crust:
1/3 cup cold lard, cut up
1 cup flour (cold)
2 to 3 Tb. ice-cold water

Filling:
4 cups rhubarb, cut small
1 1/4 cups sugar
1/3 cup flour

Topping:
1 cup flour (cold)
1/2 cup brown sugar
1 stick cold butter, cut up

To make the crust, mix lard and flour in food processor with steel blade until mixture resembles coarse meal. Add water gradually until mixture just starts to form a ball.

To prepare rhubarb for filling, cut the stalks into 1/4-inch pieces cut lengthwise, which makes for a very tender pie with a nice

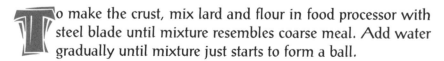

texture. Mix together the rhubarb, sugar and flour in a bowl until sugar starts to dissolve and coats the rhubarb evenly.

For the topping, mix flour and brown sugar in food processor with steel blade. Add butter pieces and process until crumbly.

Roll crust so it fits in 10-inch pie plate. Add filling and then topping, and bake at 400°F for one hour. The pie is done when the filling just starts to bubble. The center will also rise slightly when done. This settles down after you take it out of the oven and it starts to cool. Serves 8.

CHOCOLATE DREAM PIE

Dorothy Rutherford, The Shepherd's Inn
Mile 72 Alaska Highway

1 cup less 2 Tb. flour
1/2 cup butter, at room temperature
21/2 oz. finely chopped walnuts
8 oz. cream cheese, at room temperature
3/4 cup icing sugar
3/4 cup whipped cream
6 oz. instant chocolate pudding mix
2 cups plus 2 Tb. milk
whipped cream and nuts as desired

lend flour and butter with pastry blender; add nuts. Press into a 10-inch pie pan and bake at 325°F until golden brown. Chill.

Blend cheese and icing sugar together; gently fold in the whipped cream. Put into chilled pie crust.

Beat pudding mix and milk until mixture thickens and turns from a dark-chocolate color to a milk-chocolate color. Pour over cheese mixture immediately; chill. Serve with whipped cream and nuts. Serves 10.

COCONUT CREAM PIE

Harmke DeBruin, Spirit Lake Wilderness Resort
Mile 72.3 Klondike Highway

1 liter (approx. 1 qt.) **milk**
1 400-ml (12-oz.) can **coconut milk**
²/₃ cup **sugar**
4 **egg yolks**
²/₃ cup **cornstarch**
⁴/₅ cup **coconut crumbs**
baked pie shell
whipped cream

In a regular pot mix together milk, coconut milk, sugar, egg yolks and cornstarch. Stir over medium heat until it thickens. Add coconut crumbs and stir. Put in pie shell and let it cool down. When it is cold enough, decorate it with whipped cream.

FLAPPER PIE

Gay Frocklage, 40 Mile Flats, Iskut

2 cups milk
¼ cup sugar
2 Tb. cornstarch
2 egg yolks
1 tsp. vanilla
8- or 9-inch graham cracker OR Oreo Cookie crust
   (save 4 Tb. for topping)
meringue or whipped topping

In a double boiler, or a saucepan over medium heat, mix together milk, sugar and cornstarch. Blend well. Add egg yolk, and cook and stir until thick. Remove from heat and mix in vanilla. Pour into crust and top with meringue or whipped topping. Sprinkle reserved crust crumbs over the top. Serves 8.

THE LODGE
RHUBARB CRISP PIE

M.M. Clay, Sportsman's Kispiox Lodge, Hazelton

"I make the topping for this pie in ice cream bucket amounts and freeze it to use when needed. The amount in the recipe is probably enough for 8 or more pies."

Uncooked pastry shell
3 to 4 cups diced rhubarb (enough to fill the pie shell)
1¹/₂ cups sugar
4 eggs
¹/₄ cup flour
¹/₄ tsp. salt
¹/₄ to ¹/₂ cup heavy cream

Topping:

4 cups rolled oats	**3 cups flour**
3 cups brown sugar	**1 lb. butter or margarine**

Fill the pastry shell with rhubarb. Mix together sugar, eggs, flour, salt and cream, and pour over rhubarb. Bake at 425°F for 20 minutes. Mix together oats, brown sugar and flour; cut in butter. When rhubarb mixture is finished baking, pour enough of the oat mixture on top of the rhubarb to amply cover. Freeze the remaining topping for future use. Return pie to oven and bake at 350°F for 40 to 50 minutes until brown. Pie should feel solid in the center when gently pressed with fingertips.

ROSEHIP TORTE

Carla Pitzel, Hawkins House Bed & Breakfast, Whitehorse

"This is our signature cake. Many people have asked me for the recipe, so here it is! I traditionally make this cake with rosehip jelly, but any jelly will do. Be careful slicing this cake, it is light as a feather. A final caution: The dough must be made one day in advance.

Dough:
²/₃ cup **butter**
²/₃ cup **sugar**
¹/₂ cup **flour**
1 **egg**
1 cup **ground hazelnuts OR almonds**

Filling:
2 cups **whipping cream**
2 Tb. **icing (powdered) sugar**
1 tsp. **vanilla**

rosehip jelly (see page 214) or jelly or jam of choice
marzipan

Mix butter, sugar, flour, egg and nuts together in a bowl. Turn dough onto flat surface and knead until it makes a nice soft ball. Wrap dough in plastic, and leave it in the refrigerator for one day.

Cut 5 wax paper rounds to fit 10-inch springform pan [or 9-inch cake pan]; butter each wax paper round and place one at the bottom of the baking pan. Divide the dough into 5 equal pieces and for each layer put a mound of dough in the pan, pressing it to the edges to make a thin layer of dough. Bake each layer at 350°F for about 15 minutes. It is overdone if edges become too brown. Repeat this 5 times. Cool each cake layer and don't forget to peel off the wax paper. I once assembled the whole cake and decorated it beautifully, only to realize that I forgot the wax paper on every layer!

Whip cream until stiff. Add icing sugar and vanilla. Spread rosehip jelly on one side of each of the 5 layers of cake. On first four layers, cover the jelly or jam with equal amounts of whipped cream as you stack each layer. On the last (top) layer, cover the jelly or jam with rolled marzipan and decorate with marzipan figurines and fresh flowers.

STRAWBERRY RHUBARB PIE

Diane Debigare, Rika's Roadhouse & Landing
Mile 275 Richardson-Alaska Highway

Pie crust:
2 cups white flour
1/2 tsp. salt
2/3 cup plus 2 Tb. shortening
1/4 cup cold water

Pie filling:
1 cup water
1 cup sugar
3 Tb. plus 2 tsp. cornstarch
3 Tb. plus 2 tsp. strawberry Jello
4 cups frozen rhubarb
4 cups frozen whole strawberries

For crust, stir together flour and salt in a small mixing bowl. Cut in shortening until pieces are the size of small peas. Sprinkle the cold water over the flour, mix well until the dough forms a ball. Divide dough in half. On a lightly floured surface, roll each half into a circle. Wrap one half of the pastry around a rolling pin and unroll onto a 10-inch pie plate. Be careful not to stretch the pastry dough.

For pie filling, boil 1 cup water, sugar, cornstarch and Jello for 5

minutes. You will use 2 cups of this mixture for the pie. Pour ¹/₃ of the measured filling into the bottom of the pie shell. Add rhubarb, and pour another ¹/₃ over it. Add strawberries and pour the rest of the Jello mixture over the top. Place the top crust on the pie, trim, seal and crimp edges. Sprinkle top of pie crust lightly with sugar.

Bake at 350°F for approximately 1 hour. Crust should be golden brown. If it browns too fast, cover it with foil.

Convection oven: bake at 340°F for 1 hour, 25 minutes.

The garden behind historic Rika's Roadhouse at Big Delta State Historical Park provides vegetables for the park's Packhouse Restaurant, which serves hearty homemade soups, fresh salads and hefty sandwiches, along with desserts from its own bakery. The sod-roofed museum houses Alaskan artifacts. The roadhouse features historic rooms and a gift shop specializing in items made from Alaskan furs and gold.

SASKATOON BERRY PIE

Ramona Holcomb, Purden Lake Resort, Yellowhead Highway

Dough:
2¹/₂ cups flour
¹/₄ tsp. salt
¹/₂ tsp. baking powder
¹/₂ Tb. brown sugar

¹/₂ lb. lard
¹/₂ cup cold water
1 egg
1 Tb. vinegar

Filling:
4 cups Saskatoon berries, fresh or frozen (if unavailable,
   substitute any berry, such as blueberries)
1 cup sugar
¹/₄ cup flour
2 Tb. butter

For the pastry, mix together flour, salt, baking powder and brown sugar, then cut in lard. In a separate bowl, mix together water, egg and vinegar, then add to lard mixture, stirring well. Divide dough in half for top and bottom crusts. Roll out both on floured board. Place bottom crust in pie pan. In a bowl, mix together berries, sugar and flour. Pour mixture into pie pan and dot with butter. Cover top with pastry. Bake at 400°F for 45 minutes or until pastry is browned. Serves 6.

CHOCOLATE SAUERKRAUT CAKE

Jan Thacker
Coldfoot Services and Arctic Acres Inn, Coldfoot

2/3 cup **butter**
11/2 cup **sugar**
3 **eggs, beaten**
1/2 tsp. **salt**
1/2 cup **cocoa**
21/2 cups **flour**
1 tsp. **baking soda**
1 tsp. **baking powder**
1 cup **cold water**
11/2 tsp. **vanilla**
11/2 cup **sauerkraut (drained and chopped)**

Frosting:
3 Tb. **flour**
1 cup **milk**
1 cup **butter**
1 cup **sugar**
1 tsp. **vanilla**

Blend butter and sugar until creamy. Add eggs. Sift dry ingredients together. Add dry mixture alternately with the water to the creamed mixture. Stir in and blend the sauerkraut and vanilla. Bake at 350°F for 45 minutes in layer or loaf pans, or 30 minutes in a 9" x 13" pan.

For frosting, cook flour and milk on low heat until thick. Cover and allow to cool. Cream butter and sugar until fluffy. Add to flour-and-milk mixture. Add vanilla and beat until thick and fluffy (about 10 minutes). Spread on cake and sprinkle with nuts, if desired.

MAYONNAISE CHOCOLATE CAKE

Dee Hinson, Iron Creek Lodge
Mile 596 Alaska Highway

3 cups flour
1 1/2 cups white sugar
1/3 cup cocoa
2 1/4 tsp. baking powder
1 1/2 tsp. baking soda
1 1/2 cups mayonnaise
1 1/2 cups water
1 1/2 tsp. vanilla

Sift flour, sugar, cocoa, baking powder and soda together. Stir in mayonnaise, water and vanilla. Stir until well-blended. Bake in 9" x 13" pan for 45 minutes or 2 layer pans for 35 minutes. Top with your favorite frosting or sprinkle with powdered sugar.

CHOCOLATE POTATO CAKE

Trisha Costello, The Talkeetna Roadhouse, Talkeetna

"This is a hearty, moist cake that is even better with hand-whipped cream on top."

³/₄ cup butter
2 cups sugar
4 eggs
³/₄ cup firmly packed unseasoned mashed potatoes
³/₄ cup buttermilk
3-oz. baking chocolate, melted
2 tsp. vanilla
³/₄ tsp. baking soda
2 cups flour
1/₄ tsp. salt
1 cup nuts (optional)
whipped cream (optional)

Cream butter, and then beat in sugar until light and fluffy. Add eggs, one at a time. Combine potatoes, buttermilk, chocolate and vanilla, and add to butter mixture. Mix all the dry ingredients together and then add to wet mixture. Add the nuts last. Pour into a greased and floured 9" x 13" pan. Bake at 350°F for approximately 50 minutes.

CRANBERRY CAKE

Mt. Juneau Inn Bed & Breakfast, Juneau

1¹/₂ cups **sugar**
2 **eggs**
³/₄ cup **butter, melted and cooled**
¹/₄ cup **almond-flavored syrup**
1¹/₂ cups **flour**
2 cups **frozen cranberries**
¹/₂ cup **chopped pecans**

P reheat oven to 350°F. Grease 9-inch pan (springform pan with removable bottom works well also). Beat sugar and eggs until fluffy. Add melted butter and almond-flavored syrup; mix well. Stir in flour, cranberries and pecans. Pour batter into prepared pan and bake 1 hour.

LEMON-ON-LEMON CAKE

Jon and Nelda Osgood
Tutka Bay Wilderness Lodge, Homer

Cake:
1 box (3 oz.) lemon gelatin
1 box lemon cake mix
³/₄ cup water
³/₄ cup vegetable oil
4 eggs

Glaze:
¹/₃ cup lemon juice
2 cups powdered sugar, unsifted
2 Tb. butter, melted
1 Tb. water

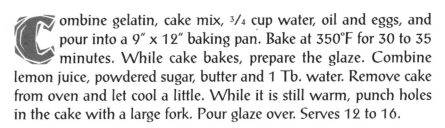

Combine gelatin, cake mix, ³/₄ cup water, oil and eggs, and pour into a 9" x 12" baking pan. Bake at 350°F for 30 to 35 minutes. While cake bakes, prepare the glaze. Combine lemon juice, powdered sugar, butter and 1 Tb. water. Remove cake from oven and let cool a little. While it is still warm, punch holes in the cake with a large fork. Pour glaze over. Serves 12 to 16.

Note: Instead of lemon cake mix, you can use yellow or white cake mix, and add 1 Tb. grated lemon peel and 2 tsp. lemon extract.

MULDROW MUD CAKE

Camp Denali and North Face Lodge, Denali National Park

"This rich, moist cake needs only a little frosting."

1¹/₂ cups **strong coffee**
¹/₄ cup **coffee-flavored liqueur**
  (or other flavored liqueur)
5 oz. **unsweetened baking chocolate**
1 cup **butter**
2 cups **sugar**
2 cups **unbleached white flour**

1 tsp. **baking soda**
¹/₄ tsp. **salt**
2 **eggs**
1 tsp. **vanilla**
baking cocoa
a chocolate glaze

Heat coffee and liqueur. Add chocolate and butter, and heat until melted, stirring frequently. When chocolate-coffee mixture is smooth, add sugar and stir until dissolved. Cool until lukewarm.

Sift together flour, baking soda and salt. Gradually add chocolate-coffee mixture, beating well after each addition to avoid lumps in the batter. Add eggs and vanilla. Beat on medium speed for 2 minutes, then turn into a Bundt pan or 10-inch springform pan with center ring that has been greased well and dusted with sifted baking cocoa. Bake at 275°F for about 1¹/₂ hours. When cool, frost with a chocolate glaze.

WILD BERRY CHEESECAKE

Deb Kremzar, Bitter Creek Cafe & Mercantile, Stewart

¹/₃ cup **margarine**
1¹/₄ cups **graham cracker crumbs**
¹/₄ cup **sugar**
2 lbs. **cream cheese**
2 cans **condensed milk**
4 **eggs**
¹/₃ cup **flour**
1 Tb. **vanilla**
¹/₂ tsp. **lemon rind**
1 can **wild berry pie filling**

Preheat oven to 300°F. Melt margarine; add crumbs and sugar. Press crumb mixture onto bottom of a 9- or 10-inch springform pan. Beat cream cheese until fluffy; add condensed milk until smooth. Beat eggs, then add to mixture. Stir in flour, vanilla and lemon rind. Mix well. Bake 1 hour or until done. Top with pie filling. Serves 12.

BAILEYS CHEESECAKE

Lisa Wax, Tsaina Lodge, Mile 34.7 Richardson Highway

"March through May, skiers from around the world gather at Tsaina Lodge, a historic roadhouse, to ski the Chugach Range. While non-skiers opt for traditional desserts, like the strawberry rhubarb pie, the skiers are focused on storing up necessary calories for another day on the mountain. Baileys Cheesecake is often chosen from a long list of decadent desserts. We accompany our cheesecake with a cup of coffee, a wood stove and stories of adventure."

Crust:
1¹/₂ cups graham cracker crumbs
¹/₄ cup sugar
¹/₃ cup melted butter

Filling:
1¹/₂ lbs. cream cheese, softened
1 cup sugar
1 cup sour cream
1 tsp. lemon juice
1 tsp. vanilla
3 eggs (at room temperature)
¹/₄ cup Baileys Irish Creme

Topping:
12 oz. semisweet chocolate chips
1 cup whipping cream

Garnish:
strawberries
powdered sugar

reheat oven to 350°F. Grease 9-inch springform pan. Combine graham cracker crumbs, sugar and butter. Press into bottom of prepared pan. Bake for 10 minutes, remove from oven and cool. Meanwhile, cream the cream cheese and sugar, then add the sour cream, lemon juice and vanilla, and mix. Add eggs, one at a time, beating after each addition. Slowly mix in Baileys Irish Creme. Pour filling into pie crust and bake for 1 hour or until middle is set. Allow to cool at room temperature, then refrigerate for at least 1 hour before adding topping. For topping, put chocolate chips and whipping cream in a double boiler and heat, stirring constantly, until chocolate chips are melted. Pour over the top of the refrigerated cheesecake. Return cheesecake to refrigerator until chocolate is set. Serve garnished with powdered sugar and fresh strawberries.

Desserts

SOURDOUGH CHOCOLATE CAKE

Sara Sears, Norlite Campground, Fairbanks

"This is one of my favorites. It was given to me by an old miner."

1/2 cup **sourdough starter**
1/4 cup **powdered milk**

1 1/2 cups **flour**	1 1/2 tsp. **baking soda**
1 cup **warm water**	1 tsp. **vanilla**
1 cup **sugar**	1 tsp. **cinnamon**
1/2 cup **butter**	2 **eggs**
1/2 tsp. **salt**	3 oz. **melted, unsweetened chocolate**

Mix together sourdough starter, powdered milk, flour and warm water, and let stand until bubbly (about 2 hours). In a separate bowl, cream together sugar, butter, salt, soda, vanilla and cinnamon, then beat in eggs. Add this mixture and unsweetened chocolate to the starter batter and mix until blended. Bake at 350°F in a greased and floured 9" x 13" pan for about 25 to 30 minutes, or until a toothpick inserted in the center comes out clean. (Excerpted with permission from "Sara's Sourdough Secrets.")

SAXON SHORT CAKE

Carla Pitzel, Hawkins House Bed and Breakfast, Whitehorse

"This recipe is my all-time favorite. It tastes very good, and it is very quick. It is the only 3-ingredient cake I know. It comes from my mother-in-law, Agnes Umbrich, and it is a traditional recipe from her village in Transylvania, Rumania."

For this recipe you will need a deep cake pan with fluted sides that also rims the top of the cake, like a torte. Carla refers to it as a shortcake pan, but these are also called flan pans.

4 **eggs**, separated	1 large banana
4 Tb. vanilla sugar*	fresh berries
4 Tb. flour	sweetened whipped cream

Preheat oven to 400°F. Beat egg whites in a small bowl until stiff, then transfer to a large bowl. Beat egg yolks in a small bowl with sugar until thick and pale yellow in color. Pour yolk mixture over egg whites and mix well; there should be no lumps of meringue. Fold in flour. Spoon into buttered cake pan. Bake in oven at 400°F for 10 minutes, then at 350°F for 20 minutes.

When cake is cooled, remove from pan. Cut a large banana lengthwise into 4 slices. Curve the banana slices along the inside rim on top of the cake. Cover the center of the cake with fresh berries. Top the whole works with sweetened whipped cream.

*Vanilla sugar is found in German specialty stores. If it is not available, use regular sugar and add 1/2 tsp. of vanilla to the beaten egg yolks.

BEAR PAW COOKIES

Barbara Jean, Mackintosh Lodge
Mile 1022 Alaska Highway

1/2 cup **soft butter or margarine**
1 cup **sugar**
1 **egg**
1/2 cup **cocoa**
1/4 cup **milk**
1 tsp. vanilla
1 3/4 cups **flour**
1 tsp. **baking powder**
1/2 tsp. **salt**
1 cup **chocolate chips**
3 **half cashews per cookie**

Cream butter and sugar together. Beat in egg. Stir in cocoa, milk and vanilla. Stir flour, baking powder and salt together and add chocolate chips. Mix well. Drop by spoonfuls onto greased pan. Stick cashews in cookie dough for claw effect. Bake at 375°F for 10 to 12 minutes. Makes 3 dozen.

BIKER'S ENERGY COOKIES

Carol Rhoadis, Gracious House Lodge, Mile 82 Denali Highway

4 cups oatmeal
4 cups flour
2 tsp. baking soda
1 tsp. salt
2 cups margarine
2 cups sugar
2 cups brown sugar

4 eggs
1¹/₂ cups peanut butter
2 tsp. vanilla extract
1 cup milk
1 cup powdered sugar
4 Tb. milk or more as needed
2 cups chocolate chips

Mix oatmeal, flour, baking soda and salt. Mix margarine, sugar, brown sugar, eggs, peanut butter, vanilla and 1 cup milk in a separate bowl, and then add to dry ingredients. Place in a 16" x 20" pan, and bake at 350°F for 20 to 25 minutes. While baking, combine the powdered sugar and 4 Tb. milk to form a very thin mixture. After removing pan from oven, sprinkle cookies with chocolate chips. As they melt into the warm cookies, add the powdered-sugar-and-milk mixture over the chips. Do not cut into bars until cold. Makes 80 2-inch cookies.

FANTASY COOKIES

Deborah Marshall, Fiddlehead Restaurant, Juneau

"Martha Hopson, a baker with a flair, devised the characteristic flower shape for these cookies that makes them easy to share or savor bite by bite."

1/2 lb. butter (can substitute 1/4 lb. butter and 1/4 lb.
   margarine but not solely margarine; the butter is
   important for flavor)
1/2 cup honey
1 1/2 tsp. vanilla extract
1 cup finely ground almonds (to the consistency
   of coarse meal)
2 1/2 cups sifted unbleached white flour
1/3 cup carob chips OR semisweet chocolate chips

Preheat oven to 350°F and arrange racks so they are evenly spaced in center of oven. In a large mixing bowl, using a wooden spoon or electric mixer set on high, cream together butter and honey until light and fluffy. Beat in vanilla. With a spoon, gently cut almonds and flour into butter and honey mixture using short, straight strokes, as if making pie crust. (Do not beat or knead at this point: The delicate shortbread-like texture of the cookie would be lost.) Just before completely combined, add carob chips. Mix lightly, just until dough comes together in one ball. Do not overmix. Form dough into 1 1/2-inch balls. (An ice cream scoop works well for this purpose.) Place on ungreased cookie sheets. To give cookies the characteristic "Fiddlehead

Fantasy Cookie" shape, flatten each cookie with a rosette-iron form. (Any cookie press, the tines of a fork or the back of a table knife will work just as well.) Bake for 15 minutes, or until lightly golden and slightly puffed in center. Remove cookies from sheets and place on a wire rack to cool. To store, place cooled cookies in an airtight container and keep at room temperature for up to 1 week. Makes 36 cookies. (Excerpted with permission from "The Fiddlehead Cookbook.")

OATMEAL COCONUT COOKIES
Multicultural Heritage Centre, Stony Plain

Stony Plain's Multicultural Heritage Centre is a repository of historical archives for northern Alberta. The restaurant serves pioneer food.

2 cups **butter or margarine**
3 cups **brown sugar**
2 **eggs**
3 cups **flour**
2 tsp. **baking powder**
1 tsp. **baking soda**
1 tsp. **salt**
3 cups **rolled oats**
1½ cups **coconut**
2 tsp. **vanilla**
white sugar

Preheat oven to 350°F. In a mixing bowl, cream together butter and brown sugar. Beat in eggs. In separate bowl, sift together flour, baking powder, baking soda and salt. Add to creamed mixture. Add rolled oats, coconut and vanilla, and combine thoroughly. Shape dough into balls and place on lightly greased cookie sheets. Press balls down with a fork dipped in white sugar. Bake for 10 to 12 minutes, or until lightly browned. Makes approximately 10 dozen cookies.

THE COOKIE

Ron Holmstrom, Tiekel River Lodge
Mile 56 Richardson Highway

3 cups flour
1¹/₂ tsp. baking soda
1¹/₂ tsp. salt
1 Tb. cinnamon
1 tsp. baking powder
3 cups oatmeal
1¹/₂ cups softened margarine
³/₄ cup sugar
1¹/₄ cups brown sugar, packed
2¹/₄ tsp. vanilla
¹/₄ cup milk
2 cups raisins
1¹/₂ cups nuts
2 cups chocolate chips

Sift together flour, soda, salt, cinnamon and baking powder. Add oatmeal. In a huge bowl, cream margarine, sugars and vanilla. Add milk. Gradually add flour mixture. Add raisins, nuts and chocolate chips. Form mixture into balls by hand to make 16 to 18 huge cookies. Place on oiled cookie sheets. Bake at 375°F for 19 to 20 minutes.

LYNELL'S BLUEBERRY BUCKLE

Sharon Waisanen
Spruce Avenue Bed & Breakfast, Kenai Spur Highway

"Blueberries are abundant in August on the Kenai Peninsula. A favorite picking spot for us is Marathon Road, where we often see caribou."

1 cup flour
1¹/₂ cups quick oatmeal
1¹/₂ cups brown sugar
1 cup butter
4 cups blueberries
¹/₂ tsp. cinnamon

Mix up flour, oatmeal, sugar and butter until crumbly. Spread half of mixture into a 9" x 12" pan. Spread blueberries in pan. Sprinkle with cinnamon and remaining crumb mixture. Bake at 350°F for 30 minutes. (Excerpted with permission from "Spruce Ave. Bed & Breakfast Recipes.")

RHUBARB STRAWBERRY CRUMBLE

Carol Oberg, Casey's Bed and Breakfast, Whitehorse

"Strawberries and rhubarb both grow well here, no matter how cold the winter was. Many other fruits could be substituted with excellent results."

4 cups chopped rhubarb
1/2 cup sliced strawberries
2 Tb. lemon juice
1/4 tsp. cinnamon
3/4 cup sifted flour
1/8 tsp. salt
1/2 cup brown sugar
2/3 cup rolled oats
1/3 cup melted butter or margarine

Arrange fruit in a buttered, 2-quart casserole; sprinkle with lemon juice and cinnamon. Combine dry ingredients, then add melted butter, mix until crumbly and spread over fruit. Bake at 375°F until fruit is tender. Serve with cream or ice cream. Serves 6.

PEANUT BRITTLE

Peter Eden, Alaska Wild Berry Products, Anchorage

Alaska Wild Berry Products makes thousands of pounds of candy for residents and visitors to Anchorage and Homer. This recipe for peanut brittle yields 17¹/₂ pounds! Readers might want to consider cutting it down to fit their needs.

8 lbs. sugar
32 oz. corn syrup
1¹/₂ qts. water
5¹/₂ lbs. raw Spanish peanuts
1¹/₂ sticks butter
1¹/₂ Tb. baking soda

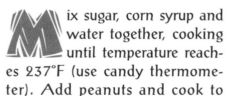

Mix sugar, corn syrup and water together, cooking until temperature reaches 237°F (use candy thermometer). Add peanuts and cook to 300°F. Mix in butter and stir until it melts. Add baking soda and mix well. Pour onto greased and lightly floured baking sheets, stretching to desired thickness. Done when cool to touch. Yields 17¹/₂ lbs.

Alaska Wild Berry Products has been making jam, jellies, sauces and juices from native Alaska berries since 1946. Headquarters is now in Anchorage, where a chocolate waterfall (pictured above) greets visitors to the Alaska Wild Berry Products factory and retail store on International Airport Road. The company introduced their popular chocolate-covered wild berry candies in 1987.

SOURDOUGH'S GOLDEN BREAD PUDDING

Jack Lewis, Sourdough Mining Co., Anchorage

4 cups diced fresh bread OR 3½ cups diced stale bread
  (bread should be measured lightly, not packed)
3 cups milk, room temperature
3 eggs
½ cup Sourdough Mining Co.'s Hot Buttered Rum Batter
¼ tsp. salt
1 tsp. vanilla
¼ cup drained, crushed pineapple
¼ cup raisins
juice and grated rind of ½ lemon
whipped cream, optional

Preheat oven to 350°F. Soak bread in milk for 15 minutes. Combine eggs, hot buttered rum batter, salt and vanilla, and beat well. Add pineapple, raisins, and lemon juice and rind. Pour over bread and stir lightly until ingredients are well-blended. Put in baking dish and bake for 45 minutes. Remove from oven when golden brown and brush lightly with additional hot buttered rum batter. Serve warm, with whipped cream if desired.

FAIRWEATHER SUNSET SORBET (MANGO & STRAWBERRY SWIRL)

Pastry Chef Lavelle Cozby, Glacier Bay Country Inn, Gustavus

Mango:
1/2 cup water
1 cup sugar
3 cups puréed mango
3 Tb. plus 1 tsp. lime juice

Strawberry:
1/2 cup water
1 cup sugar
3 cups puréed fresh or frozen strawberries
3 Tb. plus 1 tsp. lemon juice

fresh mint leaves

Prepare mango sorbet first. In a saucepan combine water and sugar, and bring to a boil. Stir until sugar is dissolved. Pour this syrup into a blender or food processor. Add the mango purée and lime juice, and blend until smooth. Strain through a fine strainer into a metal or glass bowl and chill, stirring occasionally to chill evenly. Freeze in an ice cream maker, following manufacturer's instructions. Remove sorbet from cannister and place in bowl in the freezer. Immediately begin the strawber-

ry sorbet. Prepare in the same manner as the mango sorbet, with strawberry and lemon juice in place of mango and lime juice. If using frozen strawberries, there is no need to chill mixture. Freeze in the ice cream maker. When done, spread strawberry sorbet evenly in a large, shallow baking pan. Remove mango sorbet from freezer (it should still be soft), spoon into a pastry bag and, placing the tip of the pastry bag through the strawberry sorbet, pipe straight, even lines of mango sorbet into the strawberry sorbet until all the mango is in the strawberry. Freeze for at least 6 to 8 hours. When ready to serve, scoop sorbet out across the mango and strawberry lines to "swirl" the colors together. Garnish with mint leaves.

GOOD LITTLE SUCKERS

Edith Macadam, Cranberry Point B&B
Mile 29.9 Klondike Highway

2 cups white flour
1/2 cup margarine
4 tsp. baking powder
3/4 to 1 cup milk

Filling:
1/2 cup margarine
1 cup white sugar
2 Tb. cinnamon

Put flour, margarine and baking powder in bowl and cut together with a pastry blender until coarse crumb consistency. Add milk until dough holds together. Roll out dough to a 8" x 12" rectangle. For filling, melt margarine in saucepan, and add sugar and cinnamon. Spread filling on dough. Roll from long side, slice in 1-inch pieces and place on cookie sheet or in muffin pan. Bake 20 minutes at 375°F and enjoy. Freezes well. Makes 1 dozen. Serves 6.

Sauces, Syrups & Preserves

The old Kantishna Roadhouse served the Kantishna mining camp that was established in 1905 at the confluence of Eureka and Moose creeks, 3 miles northwest of Wonder Lake in what is today Denali National Park and Preserve. Several mining camps appeared almost overnight when gold was discovered in the Kantishna Hills, but most were abandoned a short time later. Kantishna remained, and the new Kantishna Roadhouse—a modern log lodge located near this historic structure—now offers wilderness accommodations for tourists.

THAI BLACK BEAN SAUCE

Camp Denali and North Face Lodge, Denali National Park

Serve this sauce over baked or grilled salmon.

1 cup **dry black beans**
2 Tb. **sesame oil**
2 tsp. **minced fresh ginger**
2 tsp. **minced fresh garlic**
1/2 cup **minced red pepper**
1/2 cup **minced green pepper**
4 Tb. **honey**

4 Tb. **cider vinegar**
4 Tb. **soy sauce**
12 oz. **unsweetened pineapple juice**
pinch **cayenne pepper**
2 Tb. **cornstarch**
2 Tb. **water**

oak beans overnight covered in cold water. Drain and cover again in cold water, bring to a boil, simmer for 1½ to 2 hours. Once beans are tender, strain and run them under cold water. Heat sesame oil in a saucepan over medium heat. Add ginger, garlic, and red and green peppers to oil, and lightly sauté about 3 to 4 minutes, until peppers are slightly soft. Add all the liquid ingredients, cayenne pepper and beans. Bring to boil, then simmer 10 minutes. In a separate dish, mix cornstarch with water. Whisk mixture into the simmering sauce until it thickens. This can be made a day ahead and reheated just before serving. Reheat slowly on a trivet, as it scorches easily. Serves 8.

LOW-FAT POINT PESTO

Ila Suchy Dillon, Harmony Point Lodge, Seldovia

¹/₄ cup **walnuts**
¹/₂ cup **grated parmesan**
2 Tb. **soy sauce**
4 to 5 cloves **garlic**
1 bunch **spinach, washed and torn**
¹/₂ cup **fresh basil**
¹/₄ cup **pine nuts**

Combine walnuts, parmesan, soy sauce and garlic in food processor (fitted with metal blade) or blender. Pulse until fine. Add spinach and basil in batches, pulsing lightly between additions and taking care to leave the greens in chunks. Add 1 to 2 Tb. of water if necessary for spreading consistency. Add pine nuts. Serve with pasta or French bread. Serves 8 to 12.

IRENE'S HAM SAUCE

Jean Mellish, Nu Houston Motor Inn
Yellowhead Highway 16

²/₃ cup **white sugar**
4 tsp. **dry mustard**
1 cup **white vinegar**
2 **eggs**

Mix sugar and dry mustard together. Add vinegar and mix well. Stir in eggs. Cook all together over medium heat, stirring constantly until thick. Cool and pour into a jar. This will keep for a couple of weeks in the refrigerator. Very good with baked ham.

APPLE BUTTER

Trisha Costello, The Talkeetna Roadhouse, Talkeetna

"This recipe was given to me by my granny. I have used it here at the Roadhouse on numerous occasions with much success."

2 cups applesauce OR 4 to 5 apples
1 cup sugar
1/2 tsp. cinnamon
1/4 tsp. ground cloves
sprinkle of salt

To make your own apple sauce, peel and slice 4 to 5 apples, making sure to remove all core pieces. Cook in a large pot with a lid and just enough water to cover apple pieces. Cook until apples are soft. When cool, mash into sauce.

To make the apple butter, combine the remaining ingredients in a 9" x 13" pan, and bake in a 300°F oven, stirring occasionally, until it is thick enough to spread. It will turn a nice brown color. As it cooks, it will splatter and make a mess—best to foil the racks in your oven. When cool, transfer to jars or plastic container, and store in refrigerator. Use as a spread on peanut butter sandwiches, or as a glaze/side sauce on pork chops or ham.

CARROT MARMALADE

Valerie P. Keen, Coachouse Inn, Fort Nelson

"This is absolutely wonderful, and you can make it year-round at little cost. This recipe can be doubled or tripled."

2 cups chopped carrot
1 lemon or orange (rind and juice)
3½ cups white sugar

ix all of the above ingredients well, and let stand overnight. Boil until fruit is clear. Seal in sterilized jars. Makes 4 cups.

LOWBUSH CRANBERRY BUTTER

Jessie Marrs, Alaska's Treehouse Bed & Breakfast, Seward

1 lb. butter or margarine, softened
1/2 cup coarsely chopped raw lowbush cranberries
1/2 cup packed brown sugar
1/4 cup honey
1/4 cup ground walnuts or pecans
1/2 cup cranberry sauce
1 Tb. grated orange rind
1 tsp. grated lemon rind

Whip butter at high speed with electric mixer until pale yellow. Add cranberries, brown sugar, honey, walnuts or pecans, cranberry sauce, and orange and lemon rind, and whip until light pink. Butter can be frozen.

ROSEHIP JELLY

Carla Pitzel
Hawkins House Bed & Breakfast, Whitehorse

"I love wild rosehips! At Hawkins House we are very busy in the summer, and sometimes I miss the peak seasons for berry picking. If you miss the peak with rosehips, it's okay because they are even better after the first frost. Not only do they become sweeter, but they also become softer and easier to grind. We pick our rosehips right up to the first snowfall in October. Avoid the temptation to use domestic rosehips, they may be bigger, but they may have pesticides and fertilizers."

rosehips

sugar

1 bottle or 2 packets liquid pectin

Remove old blooms and stems from the rosehips. Boil 1 cup rosehips with 1 1/2 cups water until soft. Sieve through a jelly bag. For every 2 cups of extract, add 3 cups of sugar and 1 bottle of liquid pectin. Bring to a boil, and pour into sterilized jars. (If it doesn't set, it becomes rosehip syrup—great on pancakes and waffles!) Makes four 8-oz. glasses using 2 cups extract.

Rosa acicularis, or the prickly wild rose, is a large shrubby plant with large rosy flowers. The rose hip, an orange-red fruit, matures in August and September.

WALKABOUT TOWN RHUBARB SYRUP

Sandra Stimson, Walkabout Town B&B, Anchorage

"This syrup is wonderful on pancakes, waffles and ice cream. I like to can this syrup in 1-pint bottles and give it as gifts. The leftover rhubarb pulp can be frozen and later added to muffins as a tasty, high-fiber ingredient."

6 cups rhubarb, cut into 1-inch cubes
6 cups sugar
1 Tb. cinnamon
¹/₂ cup water (optional)

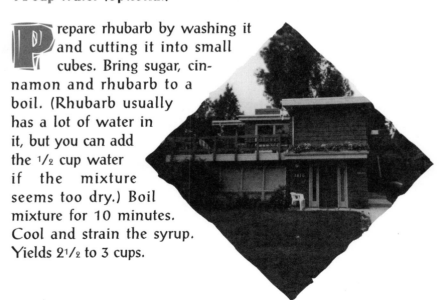

Prepare rhubarb by washing it and cutting it into small cubes. Bring sugar, cinnamon and rhubarb to a boil. (Rhubarb usually has a lot of water in it, but you can add the ¹/₂ cup water if the mixture seems too dry.) Boil mixture for 10 minutes. Cool and strain the syrup. Yields 2¹/₂ to 3 cups.

Contributors

A Fireweed Hideaway Bed and Breakfast
P.O. Box 82057, Fairbanks, AK 99708
(907) 457-2579

A Puffin's Bed and Breakfast Lodge
Box 3, Gustavus, AK 99826
(907) 697-2260 Fax (907) 697-2258

Alaska Cafe & Dining Room
Box 246, Dawson Creek, BC V1G 3T5
(250) 782-7998 Fax (250) 782-6277

Alaska Sourdough B&B
Box 812, Cooper Landing, AK 99572
(907) 595-1541 Fax (907) 595-1541

Alaska Wild Berry Products
International Airport Road, Anchorage, AK
(907) 562-8858

Alaska Wildland Adventures
HC 64 Box 26, Cooper Landing, AK 99572
(907) 595-1279 Fax (907) 595-1428

Alaska's Treehouse Bed & Breakfast
Box 861, Seward, AK 99664
(907) 224-3867 Fax (907) 224-3978

Alaskan Frontier Gardens
P.O. Box 24-1881
Anchorage, AK 99524-1881
(907) 345-6556 Fax (907) 562-2923

Almost Home Bed & Breakfast
1269 Upland Court, Homer, AK 99603
(907) 235-2553 Fax (907) 235-0553

Alyeska Resort
P.O. Box 249, Girdwood, AK 99587
(907) 754-2211 Fax (907) 754-2290

Applesauce Inn Bed & Breakfast
P.O. Box 10355, Fairbanks, AK 99712
(907) 457-3392 Fax (907) 457-3332

Arctic Fox Inn
326 E. 2nd Court, Anchorage, AK 99501
(907) 272-4818 Fax (907) 272-4819

At Schnell's Bed and Breakfast
6608 Chevigny, Anchorage, AK 99502
(907) 243-2074

Bed & Breakfast Inn Margaree
933-111 Ave., Dawson Creek, BC V1G 2X4
(250) 782-4319

Bed & Breakfast On The Park
602 West 10th Ave., Anchorage, AK 99501
(907) 277-0878

Birch Boy Products
P.O. Box 637, Haines, AK 99827
(907) 767-5660

Birch Grove Inn Bed and Breakfast
P.O. Box 81387, Fairbanks, AK 99708
(907) 479-5781 Fax (907) 479-5781

Birch Haven Inn Bed and Breakfast
233 Fairhill Road, Fairbanks, AK 99712
(907) 457-2451 Fax (907) 457-2452

Bitter Creek Cafe & Mercantile
Box 975, Stewart, BC V0T 1W0
(250) 636-2166

Blueberry Lodge
9436 N. Douglas Highway
Juneau, AK 99801
(907) 463-5886 Fax (907) 463-5886

The Blue Goose Bed & Breakfast
4466 Dartmouth, Fairbanks, AK 99709
(907) 479-6973 Fax (907) 457-6973

The Blues Moose Cafe, Yukon Inn
4220 4th Avenue, Whitehorse, YT Y1A 1K1
(403) 667-2527 Fax (403) 668-7643

The Bluff House Bed & Breakfast
P.O. Box 39327, Ninilchik, AK 99639
(907) 567-3605

Brigitte's Bavarian Bed & Breakfast
P.O. Box 2391, Homer, AK 99603
(907) 235-6620

The Cabin Bed & Breakfast
Box 5334, Haines Junction, YT Y0B 1L0
(403) 634-2626 Fax (403) 634-2626

Casey's Bed and Breakfast
608 Wood Street, Whitehorse, YT Y1A 2G3
(403) 668-7481

Cedar Creek Vacation Home
P.O. Box 10355, Fairbanks, AK 99712
(907) 457-3392 Fax (907) 457-3332

Cedarvale Cafe
P.O. Box 435, Cedarvale, BC V0J 2A0
(250) 849-5539

The Chilket Restaurant & Bakery
P.O. Box 691, Haines, AK 99827
(907) 766-2920 Fax (907) 766-2992

Chocolate Drop B&B
P.O. Box 70, Homer, AK 99603
(907) 235-3668 Fax (907) 235-3729

Cinnamon Cache Bakery & Coffee Shop
Box 95, Carcross, YT Y0B 1B0
(403) 821-4331 Fax (403) 821-4331

Cline's Caswell Lake Bed and Breakfast
HC 89 Box 1601, Willow, AK 99688
(907) 495-1014 Fax (907) 346-2555

Coachouse Inn
Box 27, Fort Nelson, BC V0C 1R0
(250) 774-3911 Fax (250) 774-3730

Coldfoot Services, Arctic Acres Inn
P.O. Box 9041, Coldfoot, AK 99701
(907) 678-5201 Fax (907) 678-5202

Copper Center Lodge
Drawer J, Copper Center, AK 99573
(907) 822-3245 Fax (907) 822-5035

Cranberry Point B&B
240 N. Klondike Highway, Site 15
Whitehorse, YT Y1A 5W8

Dawson Peaks Resort
P.O. Box 80, Teslin, YT Y0A 1B0
(403) 390-2310 Fax (403) 390-2244

Denali National Park Wilderness Centers
Camp Denali and North Face Lodge,
P.O. Box 67, Denali Park, AK 99755
(907) 683-2290 Fax (907) 683-1568

Denali View Bed & Breakfast
HC 89 Box 8360, Talkeetna, AK 99676
(907) 733-2778 Fax (907) 733-2778

Eleanor's Northern Lights B&B
360 State Street
Fairbanks, AK 99701
(907) 452-2598

Fernbrook Bed & Breakfast
8120 Rabbit Creek Road
Anchorage, AK 99516
(907) 345-1954

The Fiddlehead Restaurant
429 W. Willoughby Ave.
Juneau, AK 99801
(907) 586-3150 Fax (907) 586-1042

Finnish Alaskan Bed & Breakfast
P.O. Box 274, Nenana, AK 99760
(907) 832-5628 Fax (907) 832-5656

Fireweed House Bed & Breakfast
8530 North Doublas Highway
Juneau, AK 99801
(907) 586-3885 Fax (907) 586-3385

Fort Nelson Heritage Museum
Alaska Highway, Fort Nelson, BC

40 Mile Flats
Box 35 , Iskut, BC V0J 1K0

Glacier Bay Country Inn
P.O. Box 5, Gustavus, AK 99826
(907) 697-2288 Fax (907) 697-2289

Gracious House Lodge
Box 88, Cantwell, AK 99729
(907) 822-7307

Gwin's Lodge
HC 64 Box 50 ,Cooper Landing, AK 99572
(907) 696-4013 Fax (907) 694-4013

H & H Lakeview Restaurant
HC 89 Box 616, Willow, AK 99688
(907) 733-2415 Fax (907) 733-2569

Harmony B&B
P.O. Box 1606, Seward, AK 99664
(907) 224-3661

Harmony Point Lodge
P.O. Box 110, Seldovia, AK 99663
(907) 234-7858 Fax (907) 234-7488

Hatcher Pass Lodge
Box 763, Palmer, AK 97645
(907) 745-5897 Fax (907) 745-1200

Hawkins House Bed and Breakfast
303 Hawkins Street
Whitehorse, YT Y1A 1X5
(403) 668-7638 Fax (403) 668-7632

Helga's B&B
P.O. Box 1885, Sitka, AK 99835
(907) 747-5497

Hell's Gate Airtram
P.O. Box 129, Hope, BC V0X 1L0
(250) 867-9277 Fax (250) 867-9279

Heritage House Restaurant
102 Carson Avenue, Quesnel, BC V2J 1B5
(907) 992-1700

Homestead House B&B
P.O. Box 39490, Ninilchik, AK 99639
(907) 567-3410 Fax (907) 567-3962

Iron Creek Lodge
Mile 596 Alaska Highway, YT Y0A 1C0
(403) 536-2266

Jan's View Bed & Breakfast
P.O. Box 32254, Juneau, AK 99803
(907) 463-5897 Fax (907) 463-5897

Journeymen's B&B
P.O. Box 3106, Homer, AK 99603
(907) 235-8238

Kantishna Roadhouse
P.O. Box 81870
Fairbanks, AK 99708
(800) 942-7420 Fax (907) 479-2611

Lake House Bed & Breakfast
P.O. Box 1499, Valdez, AK 99686
(907) 835-4752

Lake Louise Lodge
HC01 Box 11716
Glennallen, AK 99588
(907) 822-3311

Lisianski Inlet Lodge
P.O. Box 776, Pelican, AK 99832
(907) 735-2266

Longmere Lake Lodge B&B
P.O. Box 1707, Soldotna, AK 99669
(907) 262-9799 Fax (907) 262-5937

Mackintosh Lodge
Mile 1022 Alaska Highway
Haines Junction, YT Y1A 3V4
(403) 634-2301 Fax (403) 634-2302

Mae's Kitchen
Mile 147 Alaska Highway
Pink Mountain, BC V0C 2B0
(250) 772-3215

Manley Roadhouse
Manley Hot Springs, AK 99756
(907) 672-3161

Mary's McKinley View Lodge
P.O. Box 13314, Trapper Creek, AK 99683
(907) 733-1555

McKinley Foothills B&B
P.O. Box 13089, Trapper Creek, AK 99683
(907) 733-1454 Fax (907) 733-1454

Millar Street House Bed & Breakfast
1430 Millar Street, Ketchikan, AK 99901
(907) 225-1258

Moose Creek Lodge
Bag 1, Mayo, YT Y0B 1M0

Morning Glory B&B
1015 Larkspur Ct., Homer, AK 99603
(907) 235-8084

Mt. Juneau Inn Bed & Breakfast
1801 Old Glacier Highway
Juneau, AK 99801
(907) 463-5855 Fax (907) 463-5423

Multicultural Heritage Centre
P.O. Box 908
Stony Plain, AB T0E 2G0

The Noland House
Box 135, Atlin, BC V0W 1A0
(250) 651-7585 Fax (250) 651-7585

Norlite Campground
1660 Peger Road, Fairbanks, AK 99709
(907) 474-0206 Fax (907) 474-0992

North Country Castle Bed & Breakfast
P.O. Box 111876, Anchorage, AK 99511
(907) 345-7296

North Pole Coffee House
220 Park Way, North Pole, AK 99705
(907) 488-7190 Fax (907) 488-5765

The Northern Beaver Post
P.O. Box 9, Watson Lake, YT Y0A 1C0
(403) 536-2307 Fax (403) 536-7667

Nu Houston Motor Inn
P.O. Box 1110, Houston, BC V0J 1Z0
(250) 845-7112 Fax (250) 845-3580

Paxson Lodge
Paxson, AK 99737
(907) 822-3330

Purden Lake Resort
P.O. Box 1239, Prince George, BC V2L 4V3
(907) 565-7777

Red Salmon Guest House
P.O. Box 725, Cooper Landing, AK 99572
(907) 595-1733 Fax (907) 595-1533

Reindeer Mountain Lodge
P.O. Box 7, Cantwell, AK 99729
(907) 768-2420 Fax (907) 768-2942

Reluctant Fisherman Inn
Box 150, Cordova, AK 99574
(907) 424-3272

Rika's Roadhouse and Landing
P.O. Box 1229, Delta Junction, AK 99737
(907) 895-4938

Rock Creek Bed & Breakfast
HC1 Box 3450, Healy, AK 99743
(907) 683-2676

Rose's Forget-Me-Not B&B
502 Monroe Street, Fairbanks, AK 99701
(907) 456-5734 Fax (907) 456-2907

Sgt. Preston's Lodge
Box 538, Skagway, AK 99840
(907) 983-2521

7 Gables Inn
P.O. Box 80488, Fairbanks, AK 99708
(907) 479-0751 Fax (907) 479-2229

Sheep Mountain Lodge
HC 03 Box 8490, Palmer, AK 99645
(907) 745-5121 Fax (907) 745-5120

The Shepherd's Inn
P.O. Box 6425
Fort St. John, BC V1J 4H8
(250) 827-3671

Snowline Bed & Breakfast
11101 Snowline Drive
Anchorage, AK 99516
(907) 346-1631

Soldotna Inn
35041 Kenai Spur Highway
Soldotna, AK 99669
(907) 262-9165

Sourdough Mining Company
International Airport Road, Anchorage, AK
(907) 563-2272 Fax (907) 345-8570

Sourdough Paul's Bed and Breakfast
P.O. Box 372, Palmer, AK 99645
(888) 287-7002

Spirit Lake Wilderness Resort
Mile 72.3 Klondike Highway
Carcross, YT Y0B 1B0
(403) 821-4337 Fax (403) 821-4337

Sportsman Inn
Box 88, Pink Mountain, BC V0C 2B0
(250) 772-3220

Sportsman's Kispiox Lodge
Box 2541 RR 1, Hazelton, BC V0J 1Y0
(250) 842-6455 Fax (250) 842-6455

Spruce Avenue Bed & Breakfast
35985 Pioneer Drive, Soldotna, AK 99669
(907) 262-9833 Fax (907) 262-9833

The Talkeetna Roadhouse
P.O. Box 604M, Talkeetna, AK 99676
(907) 733-1351

Tiekel River Lodge
SR Box 110, Valdez, AK 99686
(907) 822-3259

Trapper Creek Inn & General Store
P.O. Box 13209
Trapper Creek, AK 99683
(907) 733-2302 Fax (907) 733-1002

Trapper John's Bed & Breakfast
P.O. Box 243, Talkeetna, AK 99676
(907) 733-2354 Fax (907) 733-2354

Tsaina Lodge
Box 80, Valdez, AK 99686
(907)835-3500 Fax (907)835-5661

Turnagain House
P.O. Box 112916, Anchorage, AK 99511
(907) 653-7500

Tutka Bay Lodge
Box 960, Homer, AK 99603
(907) 235-3905

Two Choice Cafe
Box 419, Nenana, AK 99760
(907) 832-1010 Fax (907) 832-5556

Victorian Heights Bed & Breakfast
P.O. Box 2363, Homer, AK 99603
(907) 235-6357 Fax (907) 235-6357

Walkabout Town B&B
1610 "E" Street, Anchorage, AK 99501
(907) 279-7808 Fax (907) 258-3657

Wintel's Bed & Breakfast
P.O. Box 2812, Kodiak, AK 99615
(907) 486-6935

Recipe Index

Appetizers
Boursin Au Poivre 56
Crab-stuffed Mushrooms 53
Deep-fried Fiddleheads
in Beer Batter 54
Guest House Special 58
Swiss Cheese Fondue 52
Turnagain House Mushrooms 57

Beef
Arctic Dip Sandwich 148
Beef or Vegetable Lasagna 168
California Meat Claw 150
Dawson Peaks Beef Burritos 149
Filet of Beef, Three Tomato Crudité 154
Heritage House Stew 153
Paprika Beef Rolls 156
Swiss Steak 157

Berries
Alaska Cranberry Muffins 76
Craisin Puffin Muffins 77
Cranberry Banana Bread/Muffins 78
Cranberry Cake 186
Dot's Famous Raspberry Scones 100
Fairweather Sunset Sorbet 204
Lowbush Cranberry Butter 213
Lynell's Blueberry Buckle 200
Raspberry-Rhubarb Spiced Punch 61
Rhubarb Strawberry Crumble 201
Saskatoon Berry Pie 182
Sourdough Blueberry Muffins 85
Strawberry Rhubarb Pie 180
Wild Berry Cheesecake 189

Beverages
Cranberry Mint Punch 60
Mulled Wine 62
Orange Juice Special 63
Raspberry-Rhubarb Spiced Punch 61

Breads (see also Cinnamon Rolls, Rolls and Scones)
Alaska Backpack Mountain Bread 66
Bannock 103
Breakfast Turnovers 36
Cranberry Banana Bread/Muffins 78
Lake House B&B Bubble Bread 68

"Nuts about Banana" Bread 67
Overnight Coffee Cake 106
Shirley's Herb Foccacia 70
Sourdough French Bread 71
Sourdough Paul's
Banana Nut Bread 74
Sweet Bear Claw 104
Two-Tone Bread 72

Cakes
Baileys Cheesecake 190
Chocolate Potato Cake 185
Chocolate Sauerkraut Cake 183
Sourdough Chocolate Cake 192
Cranberry Cake 186
Lemon-on-Lemon Cake 187
Mayonnaise Chocolate Cake 184
Muldrow Mud Cake 188
Saxon Short Cake 193
Sourdough Chocolate Cake 192
Wild Berry Cheesecake 189

Cereals
Almost Famous Granola 8
Good Morning Granola 10
Helga's Hot Cereal 11

Cheese
Boursin Au Poivre 56
Cheese Scones 99
Fireweed Quiche 33
Guest House Special 58
Ham and Cheese Florentine 41
Herbed Ham and Cheese Bake 43
Sausage-Cheese Breakfast Strata 49
Swiss Cheese Fondue 52

Chicken (see Poultry)

Chili
Copper River King Salmon Chili 140
North Pole Coffee's Famous Chili 167

Cinnamon rolls
Easy Cinnamon Rolls 92
Frosted Cinnamon Rolls 94
Overnight Cinnamon Rolls 93
Sourdough Cinnamon Rolls 98
Victorian Heights
Cinnamon Rolls 97

Cookies

Bear Paw Cookies 194
Biker's Energy Cookies 195
The Cookie 199
Fantasy Cookies 196
Good Little Suckers 206
Oatmeal Coconut Cookies 198

Crab

Crab Cakes 145
Crab-stuffed Mushrooms 53
Halibut Mornay 133
Pepper Crab Cakes 146

Desserts (see also Cakes, Candy, Cookies and Pies)

Fairweather Sunset Sorbet 204
Lynell's Blueberry Buckle 200
Peanut Brittle 202
Rhubarb Strawberry Crumble 201
Sourdough's Golden Bread
 Pudding 203

Egg dishes

Alaskan Sourdough Smoked
 Yukon King Salmon Omelet 30
Breakfast Turnovers 36
Chocolate Drop B&B's Sausage Strata 48
Easy Egg Soufflé 37
Easy Egg Surprise 38
Easy Garden Quiche 31
Easy Spinach Quiche 32
Eggs Marvelous 39
Fiesta Brunch 40
Fireweed Quiche 33
Gables Frittata 35
Ham and Cheese Florentine 41
Heavenly French Custard 42
Herbed Ham and Cheese Bake 43
McKinley Breakfast 44
My Dad's Baked Eggs 45
North Country Glacier Melter 46
Salmon Quiche 34
Sausage Strata Eleanor 47
Sausage-Cheese Breakfast Strata 49
Skilak Omelet 28

French Toasts

Baked Peach French Toast 24
Fotzelschnitten 25
Freezer French Toast 26

Scotch Toast 27

Halibut

Alaskan-style Salmon
 Stuffed Halibut 130
Grilled Halibut with
 Sun-dried Tomato Sauce 132
Halibut Mornay 133
Halibut Surprise 134
Happy Halibut 135
Homestead Halibut 136
Unforgettable Halibut 137

Jams and jellies

Apple Butter 211
Carrot Marmalade 212
Rosehip Jelly 214

Meat (see Beef, Pork and Poultry)

Muffins

Alaska Cranberry Muffins 76
Craisin Puffin Muffins 77
Cranberry Banana Bread/Muffins 78
Green Apple Muffins 79
Heartstone Muffins 80
Marvelous Muffins 81
Midnight Sun Muffins 82
Mom's Muffins 83
Pumpkin Muffins 84
Sourdough Blueberry Muffins 85

Pancakes

Baked Apple Pancake 12
Banana Nut Pancakes 13
"Dream" Oven Pancake 14
Finnish Oven Pancake 15
Gingerbread Pancakes with
 Lemon Curd 16
Moose Creek Sourdough Pancakes 20
Overnight Sourdough Pancakes 17
Sausage Oven Pancake 18
Swedish Oven Pancake 19
Treehouse Signature
 Sourdough Pancakes 22

Pasta

Beef or Vegetable Lasagna 168
Point Pesto 209

Pies

Alaska Rhubarb Pie 172
Chocolate Dream Pie 174
Coconut Cream Pie 175